TWAYNE'S WORLD AUTHORS SERIES

A Survey of the World's Literature

Sylvia E. Bowman, Indiana University
GENERAL EDITOR

CANADA

Joseph Jones, University of Texas at Austin
EDITOR

John Coulter

TWAS 400

John Coulter

JOHN COULTER

By **GERALDINE ANTHONY, S.C.**
Mount Saint Vincent University
Halifax, Nova Scotia

TWAYNE PUBLISHERS

A DIVISION OF G. K. HALL & CO., BOSTON

Library of Congress Cataloging in Publication Data

Anthony, Geraldine, 1919-
   John Coulter.

   (Twayne's world authors series; TWAS 400:
Canada)
   Bibliography: p. 159–72.
   Includes index.
   1. Coulter, John, 1888-   —Criticism and
interpretation.
PR6005.0812Z57   812'.5'2   76–10728
ISBN 0–8057–6240–X

For Bill
And in memory of Ruth

Contents

About the Author

Geraldine Anthony, S. C., is general editor of *Profiles in Canadian Drama*, a series of books on Canadian dramatists published by Gage Publishers, Toronto. As associate professor of English at Mount Saint Vincent University, Halifax, she gives courses in American and Canadian literature. For several summers she taught at Hofstra University, where she gave courses in Shakespeare and in twentieth century American and British literature. Although her specialty is the seventeenth century (she has an M.A. in philosophy with a thesis on Descartes, and a Ph.D. in English with a dissertation on Dryden—both from St. John's University, New York) her chief interest lies in drama and this interest has resulted in a sabbatical year devoted entirely to research in Canadian drama. Dr. Anthony has visited almost all the centers of theater across Canada and has made the acquaintance of a number of Canadian playwrights actively engaged in writing and directing. She has published articles in the *Canadian Theatre Review, Canadian Drama/L'Art-Dramatique Canadien,* the *Canadian Library Journal,* and *Cithara.* She has been the recipient of a fellowship in journalism from the *Wall Street Journal* at the University of Minnesota and has done postdoctoral studies in seventeenth century literature at Oxford University, and in modern drama at Columbia University. A native New Yorker and a member of the Congregation of the Sisters of Charity, Dr. Anthony has been a resident of Nova Scotia since 1963.

Preface

In the field of Canadian drama, John Coulter has twice received extraordinary popular recognition: once at the beginning of his Canadian playwrighting career when he won almost every award available at the 1936 Dominion Drama Festival for his play *The House in the Quiet Glen*, the adjudicator being the renowned man of the theater, Michel Saint-Denis, and again at the end of his long literary trek when his twenty-five year old play *Riel* was given a triumphant revival performance at the National Arts Center in Ottawa in 1975. Referred to by some critics as the dean of Canadian playwrights, Coulter is one of the oldest and one of the most productive living dramatists in Canada today.

It is not hard to account for his success with *The House in the Quiet Glen*, which was presented at a time when the Canadian public was looking for something fresh and spontaneous in drama. *The House in the Quiet Glen* offered them an Ulster folk comedy with colorful characterization, racy dialogue, and authentic atmosphere. It was, besides, written by a Canadian immigrant, and, though he was an Ulsterman, he was embraced by Canadians as one of their own since he had chosen to make his home permanently in Canada.

Coulter's second outstanding triumph was the Canadian play *Riel*, an immediate success when first presented in Toronto in 1950. It had the distinction of stirring the roots of controversy, arousing the prejudices and antipathies of Canadian people once again to the French-English hostilities in the struggle for control of Canada. This play was responsible for intensive research into the history of Riel by scholars and statesmen, helping to bridge the gap between English and French Canada, and providing a national hero in the person of Manitoba's founder and Métis freedom-fighter and leader, Louis Riel. The spirit of nationalism that has since developed in

Canada is due partly to the so-called "Riel Industry" which Coulter initiated with his now famous play.

In the long period between *The House in the Quiet Glen* and the gala revival of *Riel,* Coulter worked steadily on what eventually became a large body of dramatic literature: twenty-four plays, a book of poetry, opera librettos, a novel, a biography, essays, literary criticism, and several short stories. His main contribution is in drama and the outlet for these stage plays lay in their revision for radio and, in a few cases, for television. The Canada of the 1940s and 1950s had not yet invested in live theater. Playhouses were few in number and devoted to the production of British, American, and European plays. The extraordinary proliferation of small, makeshift playhouses in every province and the increase in the writing and production of Canadian plays happened only in the 1960s, when most of Coulter's plays had already been produced on radio. As a result of the exigencies of the times in which he wrote, there exist three versions of almost all of Coulter's plays: one for the stage, one for radio, and one for television.

This study attempts to analyze Coulter's writings in the light of accepted literary and artistic norms. The remarkable fact here is that Coulter anticipated the creation of some major dramatic forms in his endeavors to find suitable vessels for his subjects. His play *Riel* was written in what is now recognized as Brecht's epic style, but before that style had actually been popularized by Brecht; Coulter's play "Sleep, My Pretty One" anticipated by a few years the theater of the absurd; "Mr. Churchill of England" exemplifies the first use of the "living newspaper" technique in Canada. Coulter did not stay with any one form. His preoccupation was mainly with "what" he wanted to say, not "how" to say it. Therefore he used whatever forms and techniques suggested themselves to him as the best method for the particular play he was writing at the moment. Most of his plays require great actors and a large cast. He never exploited the theater by presenting little comedies of two or three characters easily and inexpensively produced. Coulter's integrity made him true to his inspiration. It is interesting to note how often the trial scene and the defense make their way into Coulter's drama. This Ulsterman is entirely at home with the speech of patriotic defense.

One of Coulter's richest talents is the creation of dialogue. His empathy for language lay deep within the silently rhythmical patterns of the man's thoughts and subconscious responses to idiomatic dialogue, particularly in the Ulster plays.

In the Canadian plays Coulter has introduced characters with which contemporary society can have rapport: the leader, outcast and rebel in the person of Louis Riel; the latent lesbian in "Sketch for a Portrait"; the IRA nationalist in *The Drums Are Out;* the early unconscious protagonist for women's liberation in *The House in the Quiet Glen;* the female violator of law and order in "Green Lawns and Peacocks" and the tragic, emotional woman in "Sleep, My Pretty One." Coulter has great sensitivity for the portrayal of women.

An important point which critics have and will consider is that of Coulter's nationality. Born in Belfast in 1888, he did not come to Canada until 1936. Is he then a Canadian dramatist, that is, one whose work reflects and gives identity to the Canadian people? Is a Canadian play one which treats of Canadian subjects on Canadian soil or is it one written by a Canadian regardless of setting and subject? Is it possible for a person, not born or raised in Canada, to produce a Canadian play? Can the spirit of a country be totally absorbed by an immigrant so that he is able to create a work of art reflecting that spirit? Such controversial questions can only be answered after the reader has become completely immersed in the writer's work.

Coulter's unfortunate fate has been that his plays, for the most part, have been overlooked. The majority of his dramas have remained in a kind of limbo—either unproduced and gathering dust in the McMaster University Library archives—or produced successfully on radio or television and now lying forgotten in the CBC radio and television archives in Toronto. Professors, students, and the general public are unaware of the vast output of this writer and his contribution to Canadian literature and Canadian theater. Much of his published work is now out of print. In all fairness to John Coulter this work should be published and made available to the public for their enjoyment and to the critic for his appraisal. Only then will John Coulter's work be placed firmly in the Canadian tradition it so deserves. Perhaps this book will achieve a beginning toward this end.

GERALDINE ANTHONY, S.C.

Mount Saint Vincent University
Halifax, Nova Scotia

Acknowledgments

I am deeply grateful to John Coulter for his kindness and generosity in giving me full permission to quote from his plays and in affording me invaluable information on his life and works through interviews and correspondence, but particularly through his invitation to spend a week at Dahwamah reading his, as yet, unpublished memoirs. I also owe a debt of gratitude to his daughter, Clare Coulter, the Canadian actress, and to his friends and colleagues Mavor Moore, Herman Voaden, John Colombo, and Gordon Alderson for interviews giving me valuable insights into the man and his work. I thank the people at CBC Radio and Television Studios in Toronto, especially Robert Weaver for making the Coulter radio and television tapes available to me, and Margaret Avison for her kind assistance there. For access to the Coulter Archives I am indebted to Graham Hill, Director, and Susan Bellingham, Special Collections Librarian at Mills Memorial Library, McMaster University, Hamilton, and to Heather McCallum, Librarian of the Drama Department, Central Library, Toronto. For reading my manuscript I wish to thank Dr. Jeanne Welcher Kleinfield for her perceptive comments and suggestions, and Dr. Malcolm Ross for his encouragement.

Chronology

1888   John Coulter born in Belfast, Northern Ireland, son of Francis and Annie (Clements) Coulter.

1892–   Attended Model Primary School, Belfast.
1902

1902–   Attended School of Art and School of Technology, Belfast;
1911   won research scholarship to School of Art and Technology, Manchester University, England.

1912   Honors lecturer, Textile Design, School of Technology, Belfast.

1913–   Resident master, teaching art and English, Coleraine
1914   Academical Institution, Northern Ireland.

1914–   Resident master, Wesley College, Dublin.
1919

1917   *Conochar*, first published play.

1919   Published "Note as to the Formation of a Drama League in Ulster."

1920–   Moved to London. Contributed programs to BBC radio,
1936   London and Belfast.

1924   Editor of *The Ulster Review*, Belfast.

1925   "Sally's Chance," first produced play, BBC radio, Belfast.

1926   Published short story, "Boy at a Prayer Meeting," in *The Adelphi*.

1927–   Managing editor of John Middleton Murry's periodical, *The*
1930   *New Adelphi*.

1930   "A Tale of Old Quebec," radio play commissioned by BBC, London, for short wave transmission to Canada as salute to founding of Quebec.

1935   *The Family Portrait*, play, produced by BBC radio, Belfast.

1936   July 4, married Canadian poet and short story writer, Olive Clare Primrose.

1937 *The House in the Quiet Glen,* awards-winning play of the Dominion Drama Festival in Toronto, published by Macmillan. "Father Brady's New Pig," a play produced by the Arts and Letters Club, Toronto; *Radio Drama is Not Theatre,* CBC radio dialogue with Ivor Lewis, published by Macmillan, Toronto.

1938 First child born, Primrose, in Toronto. Moved with family to New York. Worked for CBS-WABC radio, writing "The Living History Series," produced by WABC.

1940 "Holy Manhattan," a stage play produced by The Arts and Letters Club, Toronto.

1942 Second child born, Clare Elizabeth Crieve, in Toronto. *Transit Through Fire,* libretto for CBC radio, commissioned opera, produced on CBC radio.

1943 "Mr. Churchill of England," play produced by CBC radio, 1943.

1944 Cofounder, Canadian Arts Council (now Canadian Conference of the Arts). Member of delegation presenting "Artists Brief" to Turgeon Committee, House of Commons, Ottawa, resulting in Massey Commission and formation of Canada Council.

1945 *Turf Smoke,* a novel published by Ryerson Press, Toronto.

1946 *Deirdre of the Sorrows,* libretto for CBC radio, commissioned opera, produced on CBC radio; "Oblomov," stage play, adaptation of Goncharov's novel, produced by the Arts and Letters Club, Toronto.

1946 *The Blossoming Thorn,* a book of poetry published by the Ryerson Press, Toronto.

1948 *The Drums Are Out,* stage play, produced by the Abbey Theatre, Dublin.

1950 *Riel,* a stage play, produced by New Play Society,Toronto.

1951 "Green Lawns and Peacocks," unproduced stage play. Moved with his family to London, England.

1954 "Sleep, My Pretty One," stage play. Sir Lawrence Olivier took an option on it.

1956 "Laugh, Yorick, Laugh," unproduced stage play.

1960 *The Crime of Louis Riel* and *The Trial of Louis Riel,* two plays as part of a trilogy commissioned by Canada Council for which Coulter received a Senior Arts Fellowship award.

1967   "A Capful of Pennies," stage play, produced by Central Library Theatre, Toronto; recipient of Canada Council Travel grant to attend Theatre Seminar, Abbey Theatre, Dublin.

1968   Radio and television tributes to John Coulter on the celebration of his eightieth birthday, CBC radio, Toronto, February 12. Returned with his wife to Ireland for an extended stay.

1970   "François Bigot and the Fall of Quebec," unproduced stage play, revised for radio and purchased by CBC.

1971   "God's Ulsterman," stage play, written in Ireland.

1972   Death of his wife, Olive Primrose Coulter.

1974   "In My Day," memoirs, written in Ireland, completed in 1975. "Red Hand of Ulster," radio play produced by CBC, Toronto.

1975   Triumphant revival of *Riel* in a major stage production, National Arts Centre, Ottawa.

1976   Returned to Dublin for the winter months. Engaged in editing his wife's journals.

CHAPTER 1

John Coulter's Triple Heritage

MY first view of John Coulter was as he approached me along windy Wellesley Street in Toronto in the autumn of 1974—an elderly, gaunt, dignified figure, wearing a slightly rumpled, burnished-gold corduroy jacket. He peered out at me from a severe, frowning countenance, his deep-set penetratingly sharp blue eyes, under the thick white eyebrows, critically appraising me. Suddenly I became alive to the fire in those eyes. It seemed that all the pent-up emotions of anger, fear, resentment, ache for personal losses, of frustration at the world's stupidities and his own self-deprecating ineptitudes, were smoldering there. I immediately thought of the characters in some of his plays: the haunting qualities of his tragic hero, Riel, frustrated by political complexities; the stubborn idealism of Barney Cahill, the immigrant and exile; the isolation and egoism of Edmund Kean in a philistine society. Later, while conversing with John Coulter, I gradually became aware of his acerbic wit, his somewhat disconcerting directness, his Ulster sharpness. Even later than this, there was revealed to me his other side—a gentle, shy kindliness; a warmth, humility, and dry sense of humor; a wisdom born of a wide experience of the vicissitudes of life. He spoke of the irrational and irreconcilable differences in Ulster's relations with Eire, the gloom of the idiot adult world we live in, the sadness he experienced in writing his memoirs.

I was intrigued by his open and sometimes self-depreciating comments on his plays. Referring to the plays "One Weekend in Spring" and "Sketch for a Portrait" he said, "I had forgotten their existence, and I still forget all but the titles and the sense of failure which led me to forget them."[1] And in the same letter, alluding to a rather beautiful essay on his idyllic island, Dahwamah, in Muskoka, Ontario, he wrote: "Ah, that introverted, heavily shadowed, and overcomplex web of writing in 'Muskoka Respite'! But I once went

into a cottage belonging to strangers—to beg some gas for my boat
when my supply ran down—and on the wall was a copy of M. R.
framed. I was flattered and touched to find it admired and trea-
sured."

In a letter, thanking me for taping his recent radio play, "The Red
Hand of Ulster," he commented: "I heard the "Red Hand" tape.
Meat-mincer version, but the gristle retained. I'm grateful to you
and the butchers" (March 12, 1974). Angry that his greatest play,
Riel, was never given the major performance it deserved,[2] he put on
producers this Ulsterman's curse: "Maybe when it's difficult to dis-
inter from the dust it will be done, and my ghost will hover in the
wings spitting contempt!" (February 20, 1974). It was given that
major production in Ottawa in 1975 and Coulter was present in the
flesh to savour its triumph. Coulter has shown a remarkable ability
to endure disappointments, frustrations, and obstacles of every
kind. His wife's old friend Sir Francis Meynell[3] referred to this, and
Geoffrey Sainsbury quoted him in a letter to John Coulter: "The last
time I saw my cousin, Francis Meynell, we were discussing the
frustrations dramatists were subjected to, and, when he quoted an
example it transpired he was referring to you."[4]

A passing reference to his life's frustrations reveals the wisdom of
the man in his ability to put things in perspective and reach right
priorities. In a letter to this writer on March 12, 1974, he said: "But
whatever degree of serenity I may have intermittently reached has
not been without sorrow—the major sorrow that lurks behind every
diversion and is not to be put by—as well as the passing minor sort:
disappointments and frustrations. But of these, what of them? No
man not a fool expects to escape them."

Since 1936 this dramatist has been an exile from his native Ulster.
In a letter to his friend, Ernie Thompson, cousin of Ernest Blythe,[5]
dated August 18, 1940, Coulter writes: "I've been a nomad, more or
less, since I set out on the long journey." And in referring to the
theme of his novel *Turf Smoke*, he writes "that emigrants who leave
their own country after they reach, say, twenty, are likely to remain
exiles rather than immigrants to the end of their days" (letter to
Ernest Blythe, November 25, 1949). Perhaps his most telling statement about himself came in answer to a tongue-in-cheek question
put to him by this writer in a letter, the answer to which arrived
dated April 6, 1974: "About March 17th you asked, 'And did you
wear a bit of green this day?' No, I have never, that I can remember,

worn shamrock spray or green tie on that day, being entirely antipathetic to wearing emblems in public of who I am, what I believe, what my loyalties, my private fortunes or misfortunes—being still unsure to which of these categories my Irish birth and upbringing belong."

So we shall consider John Coulter—the dramatist, author, poet, critic—the Ulsterman with deepest love for Ulster but scarcely less for Eire, the naturalized Canadian citizen with strong attachments and loyalties to Canada. In studying his contributions to Irish and Canadian literature, let us not forget John Coulter—the man.

John Coulter is perhaps the only Canadian dramatist, author, and poet directly influenced by the Irish literary renaissance. Born in Belfast, Northern Ireland, in 1888, he grew up in the time of the first Ulster dramatists and then moved to Dublin to be in touch with the intellectual excitement generated by Yeats and the Abbey Theatre. From the renowned Irish writers he imbibed much of their spirit and style. After long years of writing in Ireland and England he moved to Canada in 1936 where he made his home with brief interludes in the United States and England. Here in this virtually young country he became heir to an adopted nation's culture, history, and artistic needs. Thus in the later part of his long and productive life, John Coulter had situated himself firmly in Canada, becoming thoroughly absorbed in its theater, its problems, and its life style. Yet Coulter the Canadian had no wish ever completely to relinquish the heritage of Coulter the Ulsterman; had he not spent forty-eight of his eighty-eight years in Ireland?

I *Ireland*

Eighteen eighty-eight, the year of John Coulter's birth in Belfast, was also the year of the birth of the Pan-Celtic Society in Dublin, out of which was conceived, through the Irish Literary Society, the idea of a national Anglo-Irish literature. When Coulter was eleven years old the famous Irish Literary Theatre was established in Dublin by Yeats, Edward Martyn, and Lady Gregory. Three years later the Belfast branch of its Irish National Dramatic Company came into existence and Coulter and his friends could witness productions of such important new plays as Yeats' *Kathleen ni Houlihan*, and A. E.'s *Deirdre*. In 1904 when Coulter was a young, impressionable sixteen-year-older, living with his family in the Woodvale district of Belfast, the Ulster Literary Theatre was formally inaugurated and the first number of *Uladh,* the Northern Irish journal of the theater, was issued.

In the years that directly followed, plays were written and produced by some of Ulster's most accomplished playwrights: Lewis Purcell, the creator of the kitchen comedy, that staple of Ulster drama; Rutherford Mayne, the preserver of the Ulster idiom; Joseph Campbell, the inaugurator of the use of Northern Irish legend and Ulster folk tradition in drama; St. John Ervine, who wrote of Catholic and Protestant conflict; George Shiels, the master of comic sentiment in realistic Ulster drama. The Irish plays of John Coulter have been directly influenced by these writers. Consider, for example, Coulter's choice of *Deirdre* for his collaboration with Healey Willan in writing the libretto for the opera; Coulter's Ulster peasant drama, *The House in the Quiet Glen;* his realistic drama, *The Drums Are Out;* his nostalgic Irish play, "Holy Manhattan"; his humorous folk drama, "Clogherbann Fair"; his modern Ulster story in *The Family Portrait.* The Ulster world and its idiom, Northern Irish legend and folk tradition, conflicts between Catholic and Protestant, the kitchen comedy, sentimental and realistic drama are all to be found in his plays and all are developments of the Ulster Literary Theatre of that period.

John Coulter grew up in the midst of Catholic and Protestant riots, having been born in that area known as "no man's land" between the Roman Catholic Falls Road and the Protestant Shankill Road in Belfast. As a small boy he watched the rioting between these two factions from his bedroom window. His parents, Francis and Annie (Clements) Coulter, were intelligent, unprejudiced Protestants who imbued their five sons and two daughters with their own quiet wisdom, steady faith, and openhearted unbiased acceptance of other people's rights to their own religious persuasions. Coulter tells of those early years when he was beaten by the Catholics for being a Protestant, and by the Protestants who thought him a Catholic. In a sharply poignant story entitled "The Catholics Walk" he recalls vividly the parade of proud Catholics past his school on Saint Patrick's Day. But in the evening there would be open fighting and riots with the Protestants.

He began school at the age of four and at the end of the year at the Belfast Model School he proudly proclaimed that he was going to be an artist. Subsequent events proved him right. He gave evidence while in school of a highly intelligent mind and an artistic temperament. He had been fascinated by the work of William Morris (as evidenced later by his tapestry "Ceres") which influenced him to turn to handicrafts and textile design. As a result he went to the Belfast textile factory of Sir William Ewart and Sons. There he worked in the design room from 9:00 A.M. until 6:00 P.M.; and for a time, at his own request, he worked in the weaving sheds from 6:30 A.M. to 8:30 A.M., learning the intricate and functionally beautiful mechanism of power spinning and weaving. His experiences there can be read in such poignant stories as "Dinner Hour at the Mill." After some years at Ewart's and at the Belfast School of Art and School of Technology, at which he distinguished himself by winning various scholarships, and after receiving prizes in the National Art Competition of South Kensington, London, and having his work exhibited many times, he won a research scholarship to the University of Manchester's School of Technology and School of Art. In 1912 he obtained his first position as lecturer on the honors course of textile design at the Belfast School of Technology. The following year he became resident master and teacher of art and English at Coleraine Academical Institution, Northern Ireland.

Coulter's interest in drama began at the Belfast School of Art when he helped to stage a play for the students' dinner and dance. It was "My Kingdom for a Horse," written by the headmaster, R. A. Dawson. Coulter said that he was so excited by the experience that he decided then and there to turn from everything else and try to write plays, and, if possible, to found a small repertory theater. In Belfast he attended many productions of the Ulster Literary Theatre, and, while at the University of Manchester he went to every play at Miss Horniman's Gaiety Theatre. (This Miss Horniman was the same person who subsidized the Abbey Theatre.)

In order to be closer to the leaders of the Irish literary renaissance and the Abbey Theatre, Coulter obtained a position as teacher at Wesley College, Dublin, where he remained from 1914 to 1919. Through Oliver Gogarty's invitation he lived for a time at "Joyce's" Martello Tower at Sandy Cove. During those years he saw plays by such superb playwrights as Yeats, Padraic Colum, Lady Gregory, Lennox Robinson, Brinsley MacNamara, Desmond Fitzgerald, and the Ulsterman, St. John Ervine, besides innumerable peasant plays by Ireland's minor dramatists. Among the great actresses were his favorites, later his friends, Sara Allgood and her sister Maire O'Neill—the best Pegeen Mike, he said he had ever seen, as Sara, in *Riders to the Sea,* was infinitely the best Maurya. In his essay, "William Butler Yeats in Dublin," he recalls those days with affection. Of his two great heroes, Synge was already dead, but Yeats was living with his wife in Stephen's Green, not far from the College where Coulter was staying. Young John Coulter was then twenty-six years old. He would walk the streets always hoping to encounter Yeats. At last he was privileged to obtain an interview with him at his home. Coulter describes the appearance of the great man, the almost hypnotic effect on him by Yeats' voice and other-worldly allusions, and his sudden practical business acumen when Coulter spoke of the problems of financing a repertory theater in Belfast. On other occasions Coulter watched him at the Abbey Theatre on opening nights as he moved about, viewing the play from every possible angle, mingling with the crowd at intermissions to catch some of the criticisms, going backstage to confer with the actors.

Spurred on by the enthusiasm engendered by these experiences, Coulter went back to Belfast in 1919 with the express purpose of arousing his fellow Ulstermen to join him in raising funds to build and open a small repertory theater. Unlike the Abbey, the Ulster players had never had a theater building of their own. Coulter's aim was to provide one. He wrote and distributed his plea for an organized theater group entitled: *Note as to the Formation of a Drama League in Ulster,* "to set up throughout Ulster a system of little village theatres having a small repertory theatre in Belfast as headquarters. . . . We might succeed in founding a native school of drama. . . . I have hoped to see the whole of Ulster organized for this purpose into a series of village groups. . . . Each village will undertake the production of one play, and so, by visiting, the complete set could be performed in each village."

The idea was to create an Ulster Theatre for the continued building up of an Ulster identity with plays for, by, and about Ulster and its people. But "the troubles" flared up again! Ireland in 1920 was once more in the throes of civil conflict. Coulter, knowing that this meant farewell indefinitely to any chance of an Ulster Theatre, decided to pull up his roots and go to London.

II *England*

For the next sixteen years, London was to provide the base for Coulter's literary activities and the source of his artistic and personal inspiration. It was here that he found highly professional theater in

London's West End, here that he met and worked for John Middleton Murry, and here that he found the woman who was to be his wife and the lifelong inspiration for his art.

Living at 43A Cheyne Walk, Chelsea S. W., Coulter would each day walk to the British Museum where he spent long hours researching modern drama for his own benefit and also for a series of articles he was writing, "The Modern Drama," which he was contributing to *The Irish Times* in Dublin. He attended as many plays as he could afford in London's West End theaters. Meanwhile he did freelance writing for the BBC radio and for newspapers; he wrote essays on every imaginable subject including tennis, drama, and modern painting. From the beginning of radio broadcasting at the BBC in London, Coulter contributed to almost every type of spoken-word radio program and to some of the first feature programs. The radio versions of plays he wrote in those days have been revived many times, and two of them, *The House in the Quiet Glen* and *Family Portrait*, were included in the twelve best plays constituting a BBC retrospective drama festival covering fifteen years of productions from the Northern Ireland station. Coulter spent these sixteen years until 1936 shuttling between Belfast and London, writing for *The Belfast Telegraph, Ireland's Saturday Night*, and *Northern Whig*, and as editor of *The Ulster Review* (1925–1926), contributing to many of the first-class journals and newspapers in Great Britain and Ireland. In 1926 his famous short story "Boy at a Prayer Meeting" was published in the scholarly journal *The Adelphi* edited by John Middleton Murry. The story was nominated as one of the best short stories of the year by Edward O'Brien's editors of the annual *Short Story Anthology*. Encouraged by A. E. (George Russell), he had earlier, in Ireland, begun to write poetry and short stories. His sketches and short stories had appeared in A. E.'s *Irish Statesman*.

At this time Murry was about to cease publication of *The Adelphi* but Coulter encouraged him to change this monthly to a quarterly and to give it the title *The New Adelphi*. Murry made Coulter his managing editor and the revitalized journal became a famous London literary quarterly. It was at *The New Adelphi* editorial offices that Coulter met the Canadian poet and short story writer, Olive Clare Primrose, daughter of a great surgeon and Dean of the Faculty of Medicine at the University of Toronto, Dr. Alexander Primrose, C. B. This meeting had two major results for Coulter: he married Olive Primrose and he moved to Toronto, which was to become his permanent home. The story of their idyllic romance, wedding, and honeymoon is told with rare poignancy in Coulter's memoirs "In My Day." They were married in Toronto on July 4, 1936. Coulter fully intended to return to England with his bride but the political climate culminating in World War II changed his plans.

III *Canada*

John Coulter was known to Canadians long before he moved to Canada through the BBC shortwave radio programs transmitted around the British Empire from London. These included Coulter's feature-program series "The Home Counties" consisting of historical retrospects, folk songs, folk tales, and drama of the English home counties; it also included Coulter's "Tale of Old Quebec," commissioned by BBC, London, as a salute to the Quebec Tercentenary.

Although Canada in 1936 had not yet developed a strong tradition of native Canadian drama it was scarcely a complete dramatic wilderness. It had a long tradition of live theater beginning as early as 1604 with a French Canadian masque produced at Port Royal, Acadia, entitled "Le Théatre de Neptune," and continuing with a lively interest in theater in French Canada from the seventeenth century to the present. The first of many English speaking touring companies visited Canada in 1795. There followed an ever-increasing number of English and American companies touring Canada and bringing with them such famous actors and playwrights as Edmund Kean, Dion Boucicault, Sarah Bernhardt, Maude Adams, and a host of famous theater people. Native Canadian drama appeared in the form of melodrama and verse plays by Charles Heavysege, who established a tradition for these forms and influenced such Canadian dramatists as Wilfred Campbell and Duncan Campbell Scott. Amateur theatricals also flourished and in Ontario alone some six hundred little dramatic societies are working today, many of which can trace their origin back to the turn of the century. To serve such groups as these the Dominion Drama Festival was established in the early 1930s, a unique movement in Canada to encourage drama by promoting annual drama competitions and bringing competitors together from all the provinces across Canada. The birth of a professional theater in Canada was aided immeasurably by amateur groups.

What Coulter brought to budding Canadian writers was the example of a perfection of form, astute literary criticism, an understanding of the creative possibilities in radio through his experiences with the BBC, an appreciation of the best in drama, a sense of the creative spirit of cultural nationalism (which he found lacking in the Canada of the 1930s), a firm-set wish to establish a national theater in Canada, a wide-ranging absorption in the arts, a genuine interest in Canadian history, and a continuing desire to encourage young Canadian writers to create Canadian plays giving identity to the Canadian people. What did Canada give to John Coulter? It gave him the freedom to write in a politically uncomplicated land, a new culture to imbibe, a wide-open field in radio to explore, vast opportunities for growth in the artistic sense, an annual Dominion Drama Festival to which he could contribute, newspapers and journals ready to accept his contributions, a government willing to contribute to the arts in a material way if given the proper direction, a people eager to listen—in a word, an audience ready for this man who had been prepared by the best in Ireland and Great Britain.

He plunged immediately into writing, contributing steadily and substantially to CBC Radio, leading journals and newspapers, the Dominion Drama Festival, and other dramatic and artistic organizations for the next forty years. He studied the Canadian scene, listened at the corner drugstores for the vocabulary of the Canadian youth, the nuances of Canadian speech. Then he would write, trying to reproduce the sound and spirit of Canadians. For the first time in Canada he knew a failure that he could not overcome. This expatriate had at last been convinced that there are certain things one cannot espouse—the inbred consciousness of another people, its inimitable vocabulary and idiom, its almost indefinable spirit. The outsider can appreciate and understand these without necessarily being able to reproduce them so convincingly in drama that the audience would find it a mirror of itself. It took many years for Coulter to find a Canadian theme of sufficient universality for his talent, by which time his skills had become somewhat more polished. His immediate concern when he arrived in Canada was to write plays and literary criticism for CBC radio and to present his Irish plays for submission to the Dominion Drama Festival. His Ulster play, *The House in the Quiet Glen,* broke all records by winning all but one of the trophies and awards available at the 1937 Dominion Drama Festival at Hart House Theatre in Toronto.

Thereupon he was invited by the adjudicator, the renowed artistic director, Michel Saint Denis, to join him with John Gielgud, Bronson Albery, and Tyrone Guthrie in experimental stage productions in his London Theatre School. War, however, again proved an obstacle to Coulter's plans; World War II broke out even as Coulter had his passage booked for sailing from New York on the *Queen Mary*.

In 1938 their first child, a daughter, Primrose, was born in Toronto. Shortly afterward the Coulters moved to New York City where they stayed for three years in a studio apartment at 40 East 50th Street. This sojourn had three tangible effects on Coulter's writing career: a clearer perspective on Canada, a play later rewritten as a novel, and the opportunity to learn about television drama in its very earliest stages.

In New York he was able to consider the Canadian theater scene reflectively. He compared its rather primitive state to that of Ireland's drama before the Irish renaissance. The birth of Irish plays occurred as the result of a happy union of playwrights, on the one hand, and a receptive public, on the other. Together they founded a home and school—the Abbey Theatre in Dublin. There in the Abbey, the people of Ireland found in Irish drama their true identity. Why could not Canada do the same? Coulter, as a result of these reflections, wrote the stimulating essay, "Canadian Theatre and the Irish Exemplar" which was published in *Theatre Arts*.

Another inspiration came to him in New York while gazing down from his room high up in the Barbizon Plaza Hotel. He looked down on the roof of an apartment building and saw there an old man, possibly an immigrant, tending chickens and rabbits in an obvious attempt to recreate a bit of the old country in this atmosphere high above New York's teeming metropolis. Coulter felt an immediate empathy for this fellow exile and he set to work writing what was to develop into that immigrant play, "Holy Manhattan." Eventually it became the basis for his novel *Turf Smoke*.

During this period in New York, Coulter composed scripts for CBS-WABC radio station. As a result he was invited to observe in the experimental CBS television studios over Grand Central Station, where prolonged closed-circuit practice-programming was going on prior to transmission to the public. This was in 1939, in the first stages of television, when New Yorkers were already viewing closed-circuit television in store windows. Although the men in charge of this new venture, Gilbert Seldes and Worthington Miner, offered Coulter a contract to supply thirteen half-hour TV plays, he declined because of his aversion to what he called "treadmill professional writing." He felt lucky if ideas for even one or two new plays worth writing came alive in his imagination in the course of a year. There was also in Coulter a marked antipathy to writing plays in the first instance for radio and television drama. These were new arts and their philosophies had not yet been formulated. Coulter was of the old school: a play to him meant a stage play, and so with few exceptions he wrote his plays primarily for the stage, only subsequently adapting them for radio and television when it became apparent that Canadian theaters, devoted almost exclusively to producing great European, American, and British plays in a tradition that extended back some three hundred years, were not yet ready to produce the work of Canadian writers. Coulter was entirely successful with his radio adaptations as the frequency of their revivals proved.

In 1941, at the outbreak of the American participation in World War II, Coulter returned with his wife and daughter to Toronto where they eventually purchased a home at 9 Montclair Avenue. Again he wrote for CBC radio and various periodicals and newspapers but always he reserved time for his first interest—drama. His father-in-law owned the island Dahwamah in Muskoka, Ontario. Here in this idyllic summer home, Coulter found an ideal retreat for writing. His second daughter, Clare Elizabeth Crieve, was born in 1942. He gave her the middle name Crieve, which is *Craoibh* in Gaelic and means "the little branch." It refers to the Little Branch in the Ulster legend of the Red Branch Knights, a place-name long associated with Coulter's family. Clare speaks of those days when, as a child, she observed her father in the midst of his writing. She said he spent long hours closeted in his room working on his plays. When his young daughters wanted to borrow pencils, they were trained to knock on the door before entering. Clare remarked that when her father suddenly got an inspiration for a play, he would dash down the stairs, tell his wife, and they would discuss it for hours. Theirs was an unusually happy marriage. "Babs", as his wife was familiarly called, was also a writer of poetry and short stories, generous and unselfish in her love for her husband and children, a good companion as well as wife. She died suddenly in 1972. Coulter referred in an interview to his wife's death, saying: "When two people have lived in such unity as to have become a psychic One, the physical rending apart by death is for the survivor a psychic wound which nothing—nothing at all—can heal" (June 6, 1975).

But back in the 1940s there was so much to be done for drama in Canada! Coulter's energy and enthusiasm were at a peak. At this time he wrote some of his most successful plays and became actively engaged in the advancement of the arts in Canada. Such stimulating works as the biography, *Churchill*, and the plays, "Mr. Churchill of England," "Oblomov," and *The Drums Are Out*, were produced during this period of his life. He seemed capable of an enormous variety of activities: a lecturer on drama to various Toronto clubs, a member of the editorial board of *The Canadian Review of Music and Art*, Chairman of the Drama Committee of the *Arts and Letters Club* in Toronto, a committee formed to promote the revival of Canadian drama after the war. As a result of Coulter's efforts and that of his confreres, a retrospective series of Canadian plays—plays written by, for, and about Canada and Canadians—was mounted. Also in 1943, Coulter, with his colleagues, initiated the agitation for a national theater and theater school at a meeting of representatives from all the drama groups in Ontario, with observers from other provinces, convened by and held in the *Arts and Letters Club*. Despite Coulter's many subsequent efforts in this direction a national theater, in the sense that he envisioned it, has still to be founded.

One of his most solid contributions to the arts was the role he played in the formation of Canada Council. Coulter helped found the Canadian Arts Council (now the Canadian Conference on the Arts) after agitating for a Canadian council of the arts similar to the British Council. On June 21, 1944, Coulter was a member of the delegation of Canadian artists who presented the artists' briefs to the Turgeon Committee of the House of Commons in Ottawa. This committee on postwar reconstruction and reestablishment was designed to expand the recreational, educational, and cultural services throughout Canada. John Coulter read the summary of the artists' briefs to the members of the House of Commons. The playwright Herman Voaden said in an interview in 1973, "I can still hear the powerful, ringing tones of John's voice, impressing Sir Ernest Macmillan and the parliamentarians."[6] It was from this that the Massey Commission and Report developed, culminating finally in that solid funding base for the arts—Canada Council. It can be truthfully said that Coulter, who had urged the need to create something analogous to the British Council, was one of the founders of Canada Council in the form in which it emerged. One might even go farther by saying that Coulter was largely responsible for Canada Council in the sense and to the extent that it emerged in the particular form which he had advocated from the beginning, namely a Canadian body analogous with the British Council and CEMA, the Council for the Encouragement of Music and the Arts.

Coulter was also responsible, during the 1940s, for a revival of interest in opera in Canada. It began with his renewed desire to write poetry inspired by the sorrow he endured at the death of his close friend and father-in-law, Dr. Alexander Primrose. In 1946 Coulter published his book of poetry, *The Blossoming Thorn*. At the same time he had become involved in writing the librettos for two Canadian operas. These librettos, in verse, were commissioned by CBC radio; they were *Transit Through Fire* (1942) and *Deirdre of the Sorrows* (1946). Interestingly, these two operas recall Coulter's double heritage, Canada and Ireland. *Transit Through Fire* represents the young Canadian's emotional state as the depression ends and war begins. *Deirdre of the Sorrows* is, of course, the Celtic tale based on the heroic cycle of the Red Branch Knights of Ulster. With Healey Willan composing the music, both operas created a stir and initiated the revival of interest in the art of opera in Canada.

Another important contribution made by Coulter was his promotion of a national theater and theater school in Canada. Although it failed to materialize, despite his valiant efforts over a long period of time, there emerged instead the Stratford Shakespearean Festival. In 1951 Coulter encouraged his friend Tyrone Guthrie to agree to Tom Patterson's request and come to Canada to start the Stratford Festival in Ontario, a venture that proved highly successful both for the presentation of plays and the education of young Canadian actors. This was the unforeseen form in which, after almost a decade, fulfillment came of Guthrie's promise, made to Coulter (following that 1943 meeting, already mentioned, at the Arts and Letters Club) to promote a national theater and theater school in Canada. If Canada was not to get its national theater in the form in which it was envisioned, it did get its National Theatre School through the theatre section of the National Arts Centre in Ottawa, and its tourist-attracting Shakespearean Festival at the Ontario town which happens to be called Stratford.

It was at this time that Coulter discovered the hero and rebel of Canadian history, Louis Riel. This figure, so like the leaders of the Irish conflicts, was one with whom Coulter could truly empathize. His cause and the circumstances surrounding it were not unlike "the troubles" in Ireland. Coulter was therefore able at last to write a Canadian play that was hailed by critics as the first great historical drama in Canada. *Riel* emerged as a play that rose above the provincial and even the national to a universal level. Oppressed people in every country could relate to this drama. Although it received fairly adequate productions from its first appearance, twenty-five years later it was given the magnificent production it so truly deserved, when in January, 1975, it was presented at the National Arts Centre in Ottawa with a splendid cast and an excellent director. The success of this revival attested to its excellence.

In 1951, John Coulter returned to England with his family where they remained for six years. He had taken with him his newly-written tragic drama, "Sleep, My Pretty One." It was described by Sir Lawrence Olivier as a play reminding him of the dark power of Hedda Gabler. Olivier immediately took an option on it. It was given a rehearsed reading at Olivier's St. James Theatre, and received a Sunday evening performance at the Royal Court Theatre in London. At this time also Coulter wrote the play, "Green Lawns and Peacocks," set in Ireland with an unmistakable Ulster spirit. Strangely, he later revised it for Canada, giving it Canadian characters and setting; it was then bought for television production by CBC under the title, "While I Live." This was a unique change and represents Coulter's only attempt to transpose an Irish play into a Canadian drama.

Upon his return to Canada, Coulter was commissioned to write a Canadian historical trilogy. He added two plays, *The Crime of Louis Riel* and *The Trial of Louis Riel* to his original drama, *Riel*. *The Trial of Louis Riel* was commissioned by the Regina, Saskatchewan, Chamber of Commerce and produced on June 14, 1967, in the Ballroom of Saskatchewan House in a mock-up of the original courthouse where Riel was actually tried. It is now staged there annually throughout the summer. *The Crime of Louis Riel*, presented at the 1967 Dominion Drama Festival in London, Ontario, won the regional prize for the best Canadian play. Coulter had at last triumphed! He had written, in the Riel trilogy plays, that which Canadians acclaimed "Canadian."

Coulter's last plays deal with rogues and monomaniacs—men obsessed with their roles in life, headed for and leading others to destruction. Such were the characters: Edmund Kean, François Bigot, and Reverend McNeagh. Coulter wrote and had produced at the Central Library Theatre in Toronto in 1967 his play on the life of the great actor, Edmund Kean, entitled, "A Capful of Pennies." The following year he recreated for stage that fascinating rogue of French Canadian history, François Bigot, in the play, "François Bigot and the Fall of Quebec." Coulter's last drama returns to his Ulster soil, and the circle of his dramatic career is complete. He wrote "God's Ulsterman," consisting of two plays. The first play, entitled "Dark Days of Ancient Hate," is a short prelude to the second, and serves to remind the audience of the roots of Irish conflict in the Irish atrocities of Cromwell; the second play, "The Red Hand of Ulster," reveals today's struggles in Ireland; in it an Ian Paisley character, the Reverend McNeagh, incites violence and bloodshed. This last play was presented on CBC Radio on January 25, 1974.

Coulter has written a total of twenty-four plays, one novel, one biography, one book of poetry, the librettos for two operas, nine short stories and innumerable articles, essays, radio programs, radio feature programs, a large body of literary criticism, numerous letters, and his memoirs. This work has been collected and access can be had to it in Mills Memorial Library, McMaster University, Hamilton, Ontario. Coulter has accomplished this over a period of almost sixty years, beginning in 1917 when he published his first play, *Conochar*, in Belfast and culminating in 1975 with his memoirs, "In My Day." He has been a prolific writer, untiring in his efforts to present works of artistic worth. His adaptations of his plays for radio and television can be heard on tape and seen on closed circuit television at the CBC studios in Toronto. His plays have been produced in the Abbey Theatre, Dublin, the Group Theatre, Belfast, London's West End, Toronto, Ottawa, Regina, Halifax, Edmonton, and Vancouver. His radio and television plays have been heard and viewed in countries throughout the world.

The years immediately following his marriage seem to have been his most prolific period. From 1937 to 1950 he wrote six successful plays, the librettos for two operas, one novel, and a biography in addition to numerous articles, essays, and radio programs. The decade of the 1950s appears to have been a hiatus in his life when he wrote only three plays, none of which were produced. From 1960 to 1975 he wrote six plays, of which five were produced, and his memoirs, a long and exciting account of a rich and productive life.

In analyzing Coulter's work, I have separated the plays ethnically rather than chronologically, beginning with the Ulster plays, followed by the plays with Canadian content, and finally those plays that are neither Irish nor Canadian. Following this is a short study of the radio and television adaptations of his plays. All of Coulter's poetry—his formal book of poetry, his individual poems, the poetic librettos to the operas, and one verse play are treated together in one chapter. Finally a chapter is devoted to his nondramatic works: the short stories, essays, novel, biography, and his memoirs.

John Coulter, at eighty-eight, is still creative. He spends the winter months writing in his native Ireland, living in Dun Laoghaire in County Dublin, and the summer months at his beloved island Dahwamah in Muskoka. Coulter has indeed earned his title of Irish Canadian man of letters and dean of Canadian playwrights.

CHAPTER 2

The House in the Quiet Glen
and the Ulster Plays

JOHN Coulter's earliest memories of theater were bound inextricably with Yeats and the Irish renaissance which spanned Coulter's early life, beginning as it did with Yeats' poem "The Wanderings of Oisin" in 1889 and climaxing in 1932 with the founding of the Irish Academy of Letters. During these forty years Coulter was busy, growing up in Ulster; going to the theater; absorbing the ideas of the Belfast and Dublin playwrights, many of whom he knew personally; listening to the Ulster dialect, as folk tales were told him round turf fires in the glen beyond the Clogher Valley; writing plays of rural Ulster life; and attempting to interest the people of Ulster in setting up a circuit of village theaters centered in a permanent building and permanent company of actors in Belfast.

Coulter's heroes were Yeats and Synge, and, to a lesser degree, Rutherford Mayne. He had seen their plays in Belfast and Dublin, and he was carried along by the tide of the Irish dramatic surge, the most remarkable theater movement since the Elizabethan age. He talked to Yeats in Dublin and with Rutherford Mayne (Sam Waddell) in Belfast. Coulter considered him the best playwright of the Ulster Literary Theatre. He had first met Sam Waddell, he tells us in his memoirs, "in a stunning head-on collision during a rugger match."[1] Later on they became friends and, with his fellow director and actor of the Ulster Literary Theatre, Gerald MacNamara, author of satirical farces, he visited Coulter's attic studio in Rosemary Street, Belfast, there to discuss Ulster drama and Coulter's proposal to have it housed in a permanent building. Forrest Reid, regarded by Coulter as the best writer in Ulster, also discussed that proposal but, as Coulter says, with amused disbelief that in Ulster it could become a reality. He was also acquainted with St. John Ervine, the expatriate Belfast dramatist of whom Coulter says (in his memoirs) that, unlike the Dubliner Bernard Shaw, Ervine "never learned to ride the sermon in on the back of a joke." Actually Coulter admired Ervine's Ulster plays, especially *John Ferguson.* Ervine had read and commented unfavorably on one of Coulter's first attempts at play writing but he had added, "But one day Coulter will write a good play."

Another of Coulter's acquaintances was the poet and dramatist Joseph Campbell, of whom Coulter writes in his memoirs, "Joseph Campbell, a mountainy singer whom I had met before I left Belfast, a meeting at Knockdeane Park . . . at which I became aware of the movement to revive the Irish language." The spur to this awareness was the fact that Campbell spelled his name and pronounced it in Gaelic, "Seosamh Maccathmhaoil." Coulter followed the lead of the Irish literary renaissance in the sources to which he turned for his plays and to some extent the form he used. The Irish playwrights' main sources were mythological and historical cycles, supernatural and heroic tales, folk lore, and peasant stories. Yeats' concern for making the poetical drama a living dramatic form is also evidenced in Coulter's verse plays. In an essay written in 1938 shortly after coming to Canada, Coulter said:

It is as well to say at once that I speak of the theatre in Canada as a visiting Irishman. . . . I confess therefore, that my notion of values in the theatre was powerfully and permanently affected by years of regular attendance at the Abbey. Week by week I sat there, 'all mouth and eyes,' watching with delight and wonder while the life I knew, the dreary secular life of Irish parlors and kitchens and farms and pubs, was turned by the Abbey playwrights and players into parable, lovely and rich and lively dramatic parable. Tragic plays there were, showing the Irish to themselves as noble persons of heroic breed; and plays full of extravagant fun and high spirits, revealing us to our surprised and flattered selves as a humorous and witty race; and plays of savage satire or irony at which we stared in angry astonishment—Irish mugs in Irish mirrors. In short, nearly all the plays I saw were Irish, flowering from the soil of Ireland and deeply rooted in it. And I was naïve enough to assume that the plays of other countries were similarly rooted, that they were similarly a means, and a most potent means, for the imaginative criticism, portrayal, interpretation of national life and character![2]

Coulter is here pleading with Canadians (in 1938) to write, produce, and view Canadian plays even as the Irish did their drama and so find their identity clearly exhibited for them in their own theater.

One sees in Coulter's Ulster plays a gradual development in form, technique, and theme. From the early one-act plays he eventually expanded his drama into the three-act form. Characterization becomes richer and less stylized in the later plays; the light comedies of his early period change gradually to serious and tragic drama. Coulter's Ulster drama falls into three categories: the folk tales or peasant plays with a rural Ulster background; the comedies of modern Ireland portraying Ulster life but without the rural Ulster idiom; tragic drama depicting the violence in Northern Ireland in the 1920s and again in the 1970s.

I Folk Tales

The folk tales or, as Coulter prefers to call them, plays of the country folk, represent his first attempts at successful drama. *The House in the Quiet Glen* was written in 1925, and "Father Brady's New Pig" in 1937. *The House in the Quiet Glen* was Coulter's first produced play, presented and directed by Tyrone Guthrie on BBC radio, Belfast, in 1925 under the title, "Sally's Chance." An immediate success, it was revived many times on BBC and won an award as one of the twelve best plays to represent BBC Belfast's Retrospective Festival of fifteen years of radio drama. This play, it will be recalled, was presented at the 1937 Dominion Drama Festival in Canada as *The House in the Quiet Glen*. Adjudicated by the renowned director Michel Saint-Denis, it won all but one of the awards, breaking all records as a prize-winning play. It was presented on CBC Radio in 1940 and published by Macmillan, Toronto, in 1937.

"Father Brady's New Pig," "Clogherbann Fair," and "Pigs" were all variants of the one title. A short stage comedy, it was made from a story told to Coulter over the turf fire in the country where it happened—Fivemiletown, County Fermanagh, Ireland. Fivemiletown is at the end of the Clogher Valley and is the Clogherbann of the title. This was also the setting of *The House in the Quiet Glen*. In Irish, "Clogher," means golden stone. "Father Brady's New Pig," the first play written by Coulter in Canada, was first produced by the Arts and Letters Club in Toronto, then revised for radio under the title "Pigs" and produced on CBC in 1940, and finally presented in its original stage play form at the 1940 Dominion Drama Festival, winning an award there. Eventually it was retitled "Clogherbann

Fair" in a longer version for BBC radio, Belfast, in 1948 and produced there on the "Wednesday Matinee Program" on December
15, 1954.

Coulter's initiation into the colorful aspects of the Clogher Valley
country folk occurred when he was a small boy. His father often took
him on expeditions up Divis Mountain or Black Mountain through
the dense mountain mist and down into the Clogher Valley where
they met and talked with country people and shared the convivial
atmosphere of a turf fire. In the summers he was taken to his uncles'
farms at Tully, Kittybann, Prehen or Mountjoy East. It was through
these experiences that he heard the Ulster folk tales and listened to
the Ulster folk songs which were later to appear in his plays. He says
in his memoirs that he thoroughly understood "the prickly dourness
of my own Ulster people." He had already acquired by birth and
upbringing the nuances and vocabulary of Ulster speech, the witty
understatement, the ironic twist of words, the idiomatic dialect, and
metaphoric language that would later make his Ulster peasant plays
so endearing and successful.

The House in the Quiet Glen and "Father Brady's New Pig" were
similar in form to Lady Gregory's farces although they differed
widely in tone and idiom. Lady Gregory's farces in their slightness
of subject, droll short sentences, and occasional loquacity of some
characters are reflected in Coulter's two short plays. But the Ulster
dialect and temperament are vastly different from the southern,
soft, colorful characters she portrayed. Folk realism in both the
Dublin and Belfast theaters was well known to Coulter. He recognized it not as a deviation from Yeats' ideal, for Yeats desired that
the national theater should tell the people about their own lives—be
a mirror in which every man could see his own image—but as a
powerful medium for the expression of Irish life; and it was, of
course, Synge who gave it prestige long before Coulter wrote his
plays. Rutherford Mayne's Ulster folk plays compared favorably
with Synge's Aran Island dramas, both of whose plays Coulter had
seen and enjoyed.

The House in the Quiet Glen aroused an immediate reaction from
Tyrone Guthrie who said upon reading it: "We could have fun with
this. What a lark!"[3] Not only is this play a thoroughly amusing folk
comedy and technically a quite perfect play but it is also a sharply
realistic picture of Ulster life and character. Economical in its use of
words, it possesses charm and spontaneity. It mingles dourness and

wit, and is refreshing in its simplicity. The humor is gentle and straightforward as it depicts Ulster peasant life at its most comical. Colorful characterization, a racy dialogue, and authentic atmosphere—all combine to produce that which marks a perfect play. *The House in the Quiet Glen* deals with an indigenous theme, the old custom in the Glen of parents arranging a marriage for financial reasons, without consulting the young girl. The plot line might easily have been lifted from the comedies of Plautus via Molière, although Coulter actually heard the story in a cottage in County Tyrone over a turf fire. The familiar plot of the play in which a young girl opposes her parents' choice of an old rich husband, being already in love with that man's son, becomes distinctly Coulter's own by means of the rich eccentricity of the characters and the distinctive dialect of the Clogher Valley people.

Coulter exhibits a sure touch throughout the writing of this play, raising it to the level of good comedy. The character of Sally as a forthright, honest, courageous young woman, exhibiting cool judgment and a sharp tongue in handling the situation makes her revolt against custom credible. She is independent—an early example of women's liberation—and she has a good sense of humor. Hughie, her young lover, is a foil for her, a fearfully timid lad, terrified of his father, urging Sally to take things in hand. Furtive and uneasy, he retreats up the mountainside, ostensibly to take care of his young beasts, but actually to avoid a confrontation with his "Da." Hughie reminds one of Christy in Synge's *Playboy of the Western World,* although he lacks Christy's imagination and boastfulness.

Mrs. McCann, Sally's mother, is a kindly woman, acceding to Sally's choice once she understands the situation. Obviously the ruler of the roost, she intimidates her husband but is also diplomatic in handling the intoxicated men in the sudden turn of affairs. She has learned to keep her own counsel and is something of a schemer in her eagerness to marry off her daughter to a rich old farmer. Her sociable husband, John McCann, is easy-going, failing to get the better of a bargain, given to flattery and exaggeration, yet quick to take advantage of a new situation. He is a foil for the character of Robert Dogherty, the old widower, a vain, self-satisfied farmer, easily flattered, proud, crafty, sharp at making a bargain, stingy, and fearful of being laughed at. Dogherty is a character that makes possible the climax and denouement of the play.

The language used by Coulter is rich and living, giving reality to the drama. He molds the raw material of peasant speech into a kind of poetry, rather than mechanically reproducing it. As a result he achieves a fine harmony of thought, phrase, and character. The dialogue is swift-moving and colorful, showing the interaction between characters. It is interesting to compare the Ulster dialect with that of Dublin. The Ulster idiom is not so highly colored as, for example, Synge's peasant speech or Lady Gregory's Kiltartan English. One powerful example of Dublin dialogue is used by Coulter in the middle of the Ulster conversation. Coulter said that he had actually heard this speech in a country pub. He puts it in John's mouth as a flattering compliment to the dour, old widower, Robert: "The big, powerful limbs you have on you, Robert, as supple as a deer, and with a ginger in your eye when you cock it round on a body, the like of an eagle!"[4] Compare this with the Ulster idiom in the rest of the play. Though not half as colorful as this, the Ulster speech is nevertheless full of striking words and phrases and there is also a biblical rhythm to it. Such words and phrases as the following are typical:

Hughie: Where's herself? (1)

Hughie: You're all your lone so? (2)

Hughie: The oul' man would twig at onct I must 'a' been listenin at the door. (6)

Mrs. McCann: a man to be lookin' after, and maybe your own bits of weans. (8)

Mrs. McCann: The great gunk is waitin for oul' Robert, and indeed it's the price of him. (18)

Robert: I'm right glad to get the length. (19)

Mrs. McCann: Dear knows it's maybe a mistake my thinkin to sprancel a lightsome critter like herself with a stiff oul' agein man like Robert. (7)

Mrs. McCann: Young and lifey! (9)

John: they hear you've blued the lot of them with her. (22)

This language is a surprise to the reader and hearer, revealing as it does so much of the Ulster character, the richness of flavor, and salty tang. Rutherford Mayne was a master of this dialect and Coulter probably acquired the knack of using it from Mayne's plays which Coulter as a youth had watched avidly. There is a strength as well as a quiet charm underlying it, and somehow the whole essence of rural Ulster life springs up in this Ulster idiom. These prudent, hard-headed, bargain-making people are yet so kind and warm-hearted. The dowry is a subject for great bargaining to them. John and Robert's dialogue is a comical example of this:

> John: 'No drinkin,' says she, 'till your bargain's made.'
> Robert: Well, but you have your bargain made.
> John: Aye, but if I'd done what she'd bid me the bargain would be a different bargain.
> Robert: If that's what you're sayin' so soon. . . .
> John: No. No, Robert, I'm sayin' nothin' at all. I'm not the man to renege. What I said I said. But when herself hears that I promised you forty pound with Sally. . . .
> Robert (quiet and firm): Fifty. Fifty pound it was.
> John: Forty pound, Robert.
> Robert: Ah, g'way with you, forty pound! It was fifty. Fifty's what you said, and if you go back on it now. . . .
> John: If I said fifty, herself'll be havin' my life. But what I said I said, and I'll stand to it, Robert. . . .
> Robert: Aye you will in sang, or it's good day and good luck to you now. . . . (21, 22)

Protestant puritanism generally colors Ulster life. In Coulter's *House in the Quiet Glen* Sally tells the old widower what he should be doing at his time of life: "Readin' his Bible and sayin' his prayers. That's what would fit him better than to be comin' after a girl like me" (20). Coulter has highlighted the humor that is the essence of rural Ulster life. The Ulster kitchen comedy is the staple of Ulster drama and evokes scenes utterly different from those in Synge's, Padraic Colum's, and Lady Gregory's plays. The dour Protestantism of the North is harsher than the soft Catholic atmosphere of the South. There is a sudden barbed but brilliant kind of imagery in such Ulster phrases as:

> Sally: Ah we'll turn a ring in their noses middlin' quick. (17)
> Hughie: . . . makin' a shape to get married. (4)
> Mrs. McCann: The pair of them linkin' other, as boul as you please. (33)
> Mrs. McCann: above themselves with the drink . . . when the blood is up. (17)
> John: She'll come to heel soon enough. (25)

The vividness of such phrases as: "The kettle's plumpin" (27), "colloguin' together as thick as thieves' " (3), "the freshness 'll soon wear off you. . ." (9), "an odd cart rattlin' below round the hip o' the road" (20), as well as the Ulster ballad, reconstructed by Coulter, "She Was the Pride," and the folk melody, "The Lark in the Clear Air," both heard by Coulter as a boy, give a certain authenticity to this little drama. The combination of sharply drawn characters and genuine Ulster dialect, as well as Coulter's ingrained sense of good theater, resulted in a play that has won several awards both in Canada and Belfast. Canadians had long been exposed to authentic Irish drama in the plays presented by Irish and English touring companies. With such a background they could appreciate Coulter's play and its obvious indebtedness to the Irish dramatists. Both as a stage play and again revised for radio, *The House in the Quiet Glen* has lost none of its original freshness and spontaneity. It is not dated but continues to offer the kind of entertainment that good comedy has always provided throughout the history of theater.

"Father Brady's New Pig" (1937) is another short but delightful comedy, a slighter effort than *The House in the Quiet Glen* but nonetheless genuine in its ability to evoke authentic Ulster character and atmosphere. Written some twelve years later, it has the distinction of being the first play written by Coulter when he arrived in Canada, although there is nothing in it to warrant calling it a Canadian play. It was based on a story told to Coulter in his childhood. He writes of it in his memoirs: "It was a dramatization of a story which I had been told as true, by my father when I was a boy, and later by his brother, my Uncle James, in the glow of the turf fire at Carnagat, his farmhouse on the road to Omagh. . . ." Originally written for the annual New Year's Eve party of an elitist group of the Arts and Letters Club in Toronto, and produced in the Yonge Street Studio of Sampson Matthews, December 31, 1937, it was, in 1940, presented as the central item of a wartime revue, "Well of All Things" at Hart House Theatre, Toronto, under the title, "Pigs"; later it was revised for CBC Radio, then lengthened for BBC Belfast Radio in 1948 as "Clogherbann Fair," and under this title it was again produced on Radio Eireann, Dublin, and by the BBC in 1954.

"Father Brady's Pig" cannot claim the same dramatic success as *The House in the Quiet Glen*. It is a shorter, slighter play written with less attention to colorful phrasing and rounded characterization. However, it does retain authenticity in its simple Ulster idiom, atmosphere, background, and wit. There are the same timeless qualities of entertaining comedy in the short, swift repartee between priest and housekeeper. A living folktale, it dramatizes the abiding struggle for power between priests and their housekeepers. Coulter introduces the qualities of Ulster shrewdness and deviousness to account for the priest's success. It is the age-old problem of man versus woman—the likely outcome is for man to win since he is in authority and stronger. But the comic outcome is the culturally induced fact that housekeepers, and women in general, somehow emerge the winners. The double comic twist here is for the priest / man to borrow the housekeeper / woman's tactics. Father Brady's shrewd tactics in hiding the pig until his housekeeper has been cajoled into remorse at his apparent loss of a good bargain is the point at which Father Brady is aiming. He immediately produces the new pig in an intensely comic, climactic scene and the play ends. This comedy thus turns upon the Ulster deep-seated penchant for hard-headed business. The intensely dramatic scene is very fast-moving:

Brady: The sweetest, neatest, soundest little sow pig and due for pigging in a short while.

Brigid: She was due for pigging!

Brady: She was so, Brigid, and by the cut of her, she'll be having nine or ten little pigeens or maybe more, and everyone of them as round and soft and white as a mushroom. Ah, Brigid, Brigid, I was heart-scalded at missing her.

Brigid: (Breaking out, unable to stand it any longer.) Well if she was such a dawney little sow, Father, weren't you the fool not to buy her from Andy and fetch her here.

Brady: (Pretending first surprise and then annoyance.) Fetch her here! How would I do the like of that, after you flying at me in rages this morning, telling me I'd have to find a new housekeeper if I brought another sow pig or any other sort of pig next or near the place!

Brigid: Yirrah it's little matter of you, then, for paying heed to a foolish word I let fall.

Brady: (Sadly.) Maybe you're right, daughter, maybe you're right. I'd no call heeding your foolish word. (Shakes his head.) Ah, that darling little sow, that darling little sow.

Brigid: Quit now, Father, Quit going-on about it. You have me near as vexed as yourself that you didn't get her from Andy.

Brady: (Smiles to himself, then artfully quiet.) Is it the truth you're saying, Brigid?

Brigid: It's the truth surely.

Brady: (Chuckling slyly.) Yirra, yirra, yirra![5]

This little scene is full of sly humor. Also comic is the priest's appetite for good food and the housekeeper's shrewdness in pretending
she believes him when he feigns no appetite, because of the loss of
the pig. She puts the food away until the priest has to beg for it, on
the pretense of keeping himself sensibly alive. The sensuous description of the food further stimulates the reader's and hearer's
imagination. This scene directly precedes the dialogue about the pig
and parallels it, scoring one for the housekeeper before the priest's
final win. Again there is something universal about this interaction
and shrewd pretense that the audience can understand and relate to
their own experiences.

II *Modern Comedies*

A second type of Ulster play written by Coulter is set in modern
middle-class Belfast. *Family Portrait* (1935) and "While I Live"
(1951) are two such plays. One involves the working class; the other
describes the county gentry. Another play, "Holy Manhattan"
(1940) reflects the exiled Ulsterman's nostalgia for Northern Ireland,
since the family is fathered by an exiled Ulsterman, and the theme is
woven about his yearning to return to the old country, Holy Ireland.

Family Portrait, a stage comedy originally entitled "The Folks in
Brickfield Street," which is still Coulter's preference, was retitled
and produced by BBC Belfast Radio in 1935, published by Macmillan in 1937, and chosen in 1938 by the BBC as one of its twelve best
radio plays in fifteen years of broadcasting. It was also produced by
CBC Radio, Toronto, in 1938, under the title, "Stars of Brickfield
Street," and as a stage play at Hart House Theatre, Toronto, that
same year. In 1948 it was produced by the Group Theatre in Belfast
and had a long, successful run. Earlier it had been produced by
Lennox Robinson as an Abbey Theatre School production at the
Abbey Theatre, Dublin. In 1956 it was revised for television by Rita
Greer Allen and the title changed to "The Sponger." It made its
television debut March 6, 1956, on CBC-TV GM Theatre.

This is Coulter's first three-act play. He sustains his style
throughout with ease; there is no sense of strain in his writing. The
play proceeds naturally enough without recourse to artificial means
in staging, plot, or characterization. *Family Portrait* reminds one of
Rutherford Mayne's play, *The Turn of the Road,* in its theme of the
family's attempt to stifle the artistic impulse in their artist son in
accord with their practical Ulster business sense, encouraging him

to settle down, get a good paying job, and marry his neighborhood girl friend. The climax occurs in Coulter's drama when Alec's play is accepted for immediate production in London. The family reverse their attitude from rebuke to praise and exploitation of their celebrity son until they read the play. Horrified at what is in fact an exposé—a family portrait of themselves—they turn on him in bitterness. Coulter's denouement—the landlord's placating of the family by pointing out the positive benefits achieved, namely, fame and fortune in a work of art—is not entirely credible. Coulter's weakness in this and some of his other plays is the unbelievably quick and dramatic denouement and ending. Rather than end his play with a successful Alec going off into an unknown future, he has Alec bringing home a famous movie star to whom he is engaged, while Jennie goes off disconsolately engaged to poor Charlie. Despite this melodramatic note the play has introduced us to some genuine Ulster people and has exposed human weaknesses with which any audience can empathize.

Family Portrait is therefore a play about a play: it is Coulter's vision of working-class Belfast through the eyes of the playwright, Alec. Coulter's play is both a celebration and a criticism of life. As Sean O'Casey revealed the lower middle-class Dubliner, so Rutherford Mayne, John Coulter, and other Ulster dramatists provided the mirror for the lower middle-class Belfast man. *Family Portrait* highlights Coulter's finest talent—naturalistic dialogue sharply revealing the idiosyncrasies of his characters and providing the ground for a subtle criticism of life. The Ulster middle-class dialect differs from the colorful rural speech found in Coulter's folk plays, but it is nontheless realistic. It is the ordinary speech of Belfast with a kind of Biblical undertone and the occasional word or phrase differentiating it from English spoken elsewhere.

The characters are sharply defined. Coulter seems to have a kind of bemused tenderness for his characters, while at the same time he does not spare them the relevation of their blindnesses and superficialities. The false values of lower middle-class Ulstermen—their lack of appreciation of the arts, their sole concern for money, their puritanical Protestantism, their ignorance of social movements, their obsession with the superficial, are all explored through the characters of *Family Portrait*.

Samuel, the father of the family, is a blustering, lying poseur, a funny little man inflicting his boring elocution on others, an Ulster counterpart of Sean O'Casey's Captain Boyle in *Juno and the Paycock*. He is the same loud, strutting cock, intimidated by his wife, and given to gross lies. He never gives his playwright son, Alec, a chance. When Alec refuses the job he attempts to foist on him, Samuel says: "Holy jumpin' jenny! Did ever mortal hear the two-double o' that! But he's gone a bit too far this time. Oh aye! Tickin' us off! Tickin' us off as cockey as be damned! I'll not stand it. Be damn but I'll make the ladoh chirp a different and a humbler tune.[6] Yet after Alec achieves fame, Samuel says to the journalist who interviews him about his son: "When he was down in the mouth, we cheered him up again with words of encouragement; when it was tail's up with him we kept him up with lashin's o' praise" (68). Samuel has his Joxer Daly in the person of Uncle Dick, described by Alec in his play as, "a solemn, long-faced nanny-goat of a man. Hen-pecked. By trade a tailor, who makes ill-fittin' clothes and calls them . . . sartorial masterpieces" (107). As in *Juno and the Paycock*, these two boastful, lying drinkers provide much of the comedy. As Protestant Ulstermen, they are more straitlaced than their Dublin counterparts. Uncle Dick, in response to Samuel's offensive remarks about his tailoring says: "Ah, man, it's yourself that's bulgy at the front and your own eye that's cockly with lowerin' pints you can't afford" (53). Whereas Captain Boyle and Joxer drink without compunction and without reference to cost, Samuel and Uncle Dick drink on the sly and with some inbred Puritan-stricken consciences, for their wives have taken them rudely to task for their drinking. Aunt Ellen, "A fat and frivolous woman [who] spends her time gigglin' and gossipin' " (107) says characteristically of a current movie star: "I've been folleyin' Daffodil up for years. Every week in *Home Tattle*" (62).

The only two characters who do not come under the playwright's scalpel are Samuel's wife, Bella, and Alec's girl friend, Jennie. Bella is a wise little Ulster woman who tries to maintain peace in a chaotic household. To her son, Charlie's, ignorant remark about religion as "the dope of the workin' class," she replies, "As if everyone hasn't their own sort of dope!" (58). In the subplot of Jennie's triangular love affair with both Charlie and Alec, it is Bella who sees the truth that Alec is in love with his art while Charlie will make the more reliable husband. Jennie reminds one of Coulter's own wife (described in his memoirs), for Jennie is unselfishly forwarding Alec's career. She dreams of his eventual success on the London stage and it is to Jennie first that Alec confides the exciting news: "You were right, they've taken it, the play. Your dream has come true" (39). On her gift to him of a silver cigarette case, he promises to have inscribed; "From the girl whose dream came true" (42).

Lily and Charlie, Alec's sister and brother, are satirized by Coulter for their obsession with religion and socialism. Lily makes a statement reminiscent of Coulter's mother (see his memoirs) when she expresses her Protestant puritanical horror of theater: "Alec took the wrong way with his life and good can't come of it" (35). To an Ulsterman this is nothing short of a curse, and, if disaster follows, he will take it as the result of that curse. Charlie is a member of a local labor group who, having read some propagandist pamphlets of the party, considers himself well-informed. He talks incessantly of the proletarians and bourgeoisie although he lacks a clear understanding of the meaning of these terms. Charlie lashes out against Alec's play, saying that Alec "showed us up to the world for a pack of ignorant lunatics, arguin', fightin', lyin', schemin' " (105).

The characters in *Family Portrait* were easily recognizable to the Belfast audiences and the play was a success both on stage and radio. The popularity and the artistic qualities of this play were attested to by Rutherford Mayne who introduced it when it and Coulter's other play, *The House in the Quiet Glen*, received honors on BBC radio.

"While I Live" (1951) is a play about the county gentry of Ulster whom Coulter knew through his efforts to enlist their help in building a theater there. He tells us in his memoirs of the invitations he received to visit Mrs. Dorinda MacGregor Greer of Seapark, a large country home on the northern shore of Belfast Lough. Coulter thought of Mrs. Greer as his "Lady Gregory." Her nephew was Louis MacNeice, the poet. Here at Mrs. Greer's home, Coulter met some of the landed gentry of Northern Ireland. It was from these associations that he was inspired to write the play, "Green Lawns and Peacocks." This title was later changed to "While I Live" for a CBC Toronto radio production in 1951. The theme is reminiscent of Douglas Hume's recent play, *Lloyd George Knew My Father*, although Coulter's play was written much earlier and in contrast to Hume's clever but lighthearted comedy, is a serious play about an important social issue. Coulter's play is not dated since it is a fundamental social comment on the conflict between private amenities and a larger community project.

"While I Live" is essentially a study of the reactions of the elderly to a new way of life. Its plot is the very slight one of Sara Gregor's futile attempt to prevent a highway being built across her property. Like the biblical Judith, she decides to cut off the head of this project through every means at her disposal, even to driving her car in front of the bulldozers, but to no avail. Ending as it does with Miss Gregor pulling the blinds down, ignoring the uproar of the new highway and continuing on with her life as before, with the daily psalm, "The Lord is My Shepherd," the play has no real climax. Yet it is a very moving drama in its poignant depiction of the grand old lady and her courageous and tenacious hold on the values she sees foremost in life. Coulter has evidently gleaned his background material not only from memories of the Greer estate in Northern Ireland but also from recollections of the ceremony of life at his father-in-law's summer home in Muskoka, Ontario. The morning prayer ceremony for family, guests, and help, with Dr. Primrose's delayal of the final amen is faithfully reproduced in the Ulster home of Miss Gregor. The Gregor family could easily be upper-middle class Ontario people, although the villagers are definitely Ulstermen. It is interesting to note that this is the only Irish play of Coulter's that he revised into a Canadian play with equal success in the writing.

The characterization is adequate as Coulter manages to draw fairly rounded pictures of each of the minor as well as the major characters. The grand old lady symbolizes the values of the past whereas her grandniece, Vera, reminds one of the present. All that Miss Gregor believes in is passing, even as her life is gradually coming to a close. Her love of nature and its beauties, of the village arts and crafts, of the slow pace of life and singular peace which it brings—all this is departing with the building of the new highway which will bring in noise, speed, crowds, tourists, enterprising business, general tension, and the pressures of contemporary life. She sees that the old life with its belief in God, in authority, in class distinctions, in prestige, in patronage, in genuine care for the poor, is disappearing and being replaced in Northern Ireland by a new life based on the working class, with new ideologies of socialism and communism, the exploitation of the weak, the anonymity of the poor, the dishonesty of the unscrupulous. The aristocrat has been superseded by the rising middle-class merchant and politician in the person of Bill McNeill, a hateful opportunist who forces the villagers to accede to his wishes by threats to foreclose on their mortgaged homes. It is he who in the end brings the grand old lady, figuratively, to her knees.

Vera, the grandniece, Coulson, the road engineer, and Boyd, the village schoolmaster all regret the passing of the old order but recognize the exigencies of time and progress. Opposed to them and as their foils are elderly Clara, Miller, the old man-servant, and Canon McClatchie, the ancient parson—all faded and ineffectual representatives of the past, and ardent supporters of the grand old lady. Their conversation, reduced by Coulter economically to the minimal, vividly emphasize the change in values:

> Canon: Our peaceful countryside.
> Coulson: But a thing of the past, sir. Today, it just won't do.
> Canon: Speed today. Speed and noise. Horrible!
> Vera: Noise can be horrible. But speed! Speed's exciting.
> Sara: Speed for speed's sake!
> Coulson: *And* it gets you there—quickly.
> Canon: Why always wish to get there quickly?
> Vera: We just can't wait.
> Canon: The lost art of waiting. Waiting on the—mystery. That secret, at the core of quiet.
> Sara: (Pleased.) Dear Canon.
> Vera: But I mean—after all—we have to belong. Be part of our age. Space age. Soon we'll be taking off for the moon.
> Sara: Man's final lunacy.[7]

Minnie and Ned are the articulate villagers who love Miss Sara Gregor but need the new road to give them and their fellows employment and prosperity. Well constructed and economically written, "While I Live" is a mirror of the technological age in which we live. Although the construction of highways is scarcely a problem today, other no less formidable changes are rearranging our life style and the loss, especially to the elderly, has the same poignancy in their distress as witnessed in that of the grand old lady of Gregor Lodge.

Delight in the singing of the birds is symbolic of the grand old lady's physical change and change of character. She is not the same Sara Gregor at the end of the play. A radical change has taken place in her, and she is suddenly old and tired and ready to depart this life. At the opening of the play she is, if not young, at least very much alive, vibrant, enthusiastic, self-confident. At the end Sara has aged rapidly, becoming old, insecure, fearful, aware of her weaknesses, unable to cope. The birds signify this change. At the beginning of the play Sara describes rising in the morning to the peace and enchantment of a perfect day:

The birds were singing; all the choirs of birds far back into the countryside. I dressed and went out. The lawn was still grey with dew. I saw my footprints in the dew. Sometimes I stood quite still and closed my eyes. Listening. All the early sounds of a summer morning. The stream. The tinkle of water over the stones. . . . A coot was surprised to see me. He scurried into the sedge. Somewhere high up a lark was singing as if he was another who thought this was Paradise. I was caught up! Free of the fret and worry hanging over us. (2)

At the end of the play Sara is a disillusioned, weary, old woman:

Clara: And did you notice the birds?
Sara: Birds?
Clara: Such singing! Outdoing themselves. Blackbirds. Thrushes! Even the cuckoo!
Sara: Can't hear the cuckoo now, alas! Nor linnets. Nor wrens, nor finches. I'm getting so deaf! But then, I'm getting old. NO, no, not *getting*. I am . . . very old. But yes I am. So much slower. So quickly out of breath. Heart! The old heart! Shan't be surprised if it just suddenly decided it's had enough. A very good way to go too! (46)

"While I Live" is in a way a tribute to the past and an omen of the disruption to come when vastly overpopulated cities become places of violence and disorder with fear replacing the serenity of earlier more tranquil times.

Another play about the contemporary Ulsterman is entitled "Holy Manhattan." Although it is set in New York it is a nostalgic and rather sentimental look back at the homeland. Written in 1940 as a stage play for production at the Arts and Letters Club in Toronto, it was later revised for radio and produced by CBC under the title, "This is My Country" in 1941, and for television as "Come Back to Erin" in 1955. The stage play was revived in Toronto and Halifax in 1962. Despite this apparent popularity, "Holy Manhattan" never rises to the stature of Coulter's other Ulster plays. It was written at the time that the sentimental Irish plays, movies, and songs were at a peak of popularity in America. The characters are stereotyped, the emotion aroused is pure sentimentality, and the plot line is artificial.

There is, however, an interesting observation to be made: Coulter's exceptional gift for reproducing the Ulster dialect has followed a fascinating transformation. From the quaint rural dialect of the Ulster folk plays, to the more modernized speech of the working class Belfast plays, it has reached in "Holy Manhattan" the Irish American idiom of the immigrant. Coulter rewrote this play as the novel *Turf Smoke* in 1945 published by the Ryerson Press, Toronto, and a second edition was published in 1949 by the Talbot Press in Dublin. Its content will therefore be discussed in the chapter dealing with his prose works.

III *Tragic Drama*

The last two and perhaps the most powerful of Coulter's Ulster plays depict the bloodshed and violence in Northern Ireland. *The Drums Are Out* revolves around "the troubles" of the early 1920s, while "God's Ulsterman" seeks to define the causes and to describe the horrors of the present violence in the 1970s. These two plays make an unusual comparison, written as they were at different times in the history of Ireland's struggles. The changes that have taken place in the thinking of the people, in their attitudes toward the IRA and the police, are phenomenal.

The Drums Are Out was written in 1947 and had its world premiere at the Abbey Theatre, Dublin, on July 12, 1948. It continued to play to full houses for five weeks although scheduled for only one week. It seemed as though it could continue indefinitely but it finally had to close to make way for another scheduled play by Lennox Robinson. *The Drums Are Out* received highly favorable reviews from sixteen out of twenty reviewers. It had originally been written for the Dominion Drama Festival but Coulter was forced to withdraw it. The reason given was speciously termed by the Festival board as "production difficulties." In 1950 it finally received its first Canadian production. Canadian producers who had originally turned the play down said they did so because its theme was Irish and therefore of no interest to Canadians. Robertson Davies in his Peterborough newspaper said scathingly of these producers that since the quality of the play had now been certified for them by production at one of the world's most famous theaters, they would perhaps have confidence to risk a Canadian production. It was never performed in Ulster, in view of the violence it would cause. Producers there asked for it but Coulter refused; he feared they would have used it for partisan propaganda incitement—precisely the kind of political insanity which the play deplored. Its first Canadian production at the Dominion Drama Festival in 1950 merited for Coulter the Sir Barry Jackson trophy for the best play written by a Canadian. It was revised for CBC Radio "Wednesday Night" program, July 11, 1950, and was awarded the Irish Drama Festival prize in 1952. It was presented on CBC "Radio Showcase" on August 7, 1967, and May 4, 1969, and later revised for television, CBC-TV, Toronto, "FM Theatre" on May 4 and August 7, 1969. It was published by DePaul University Press in 1971.

Coulter wrote the play in four weeks at his summer home in Muskoka, Ontario, beginning it on June 23, 1947. He said of it in his memoirs, "It seemed to me that the language of violence had become the one in which to converse and be understood in the theatre." The time is set at the peak of "the troubles" in Belfast in that bitter period of the 1920–1921 riots when street battles between the Royal Irish Constabulary and the Irish Republican Army were rife. The action takes place in a small home between the Falls and Shankill Roads, that seething center of Catholic and Protestant confrontation, in which Coulter himself had lived as a small boy, and about which he writes in his short story "The Catholics Walk." The six main characters are typical of this type of Irish drama: Sergeant Sheridan, a Protestant policeman whose training emphasized duty to the force before family loyalties; his gentle but misguided Protestant wife; their daughter, Jean, a Dublin educated schoolteacher, secretly married to an IRA man and expecting their first child; Denis Patterson, the IRA man whose loyalty to the cause supersedes all else; Constable Nixon, a bigoted Ulsterman, jealous of Jean's love for Denis; Matt McCann, a pigeon fancier who supplies the comic element in an otherwise serious drama. Matt never becomes embroiled in "the troubles"; as he says in the contemporary Ulster idiom:

Matt: Dogs and pigeons isn't bothered with politics either. They've more sense. . . . Here lay your peepers on this beauty! As nice a wee red checker hen as you'd see in any loft in the town, eh? What do you say, Sergeant, eh? (Gives her to the Sergeant.)
Sergeant: (Holding her up and admiring her.) A nice little article. Where did you steal her from? (33)[8]

Matt is indignant, then neatly changes the subject to the sensitivity and clairvoyance of pigeons. In the last scene when the Sergeant realizes he must act from integrity and give himself up, despite his wife's telling him it is all so meaningless, Matt, the uneducated pigeon fancier, points out his own wise detachment from it all, which in fact, has been Coulter's position all along: "Oh, but I say, Sergeant—when it's all over and you've a minute's peace, don't forget to look round to the loft to see the wee blue tumbler—a beauty, Sergeant. . . . Why, man alive, she's up there now, tumbling and carrying on to her heart's content and doesn't give a damn for Tans or the Police. . . . Just like me!"(65).

The theme is a familiar one dealing with a family sharply divided by political issues. Tension is created when Sergeant Sheridan is confronted with a choice between family loyalties and the police force, involving his whole future—his job, his pension, his reputation. There is nothing new in Coulter's creation of this character, a man with an exemplary police force record who must, at the play's climax, choose between harboring a wounded IRA leader (whom he suddenly discovers to be his son-in-law), and doing his duty by turning him in. Like so many tragic characters before him, he hesitates, parries for time, precious time in which the IRA men are able to rescue their leader, and Sheridan must give himself up to his fellow constables. What is personal to Coulter in this play is his own wise and often stoically pessimistic view of Northern Ireland's "troubles." In the following excerpts he puts into Jean's head the sudden illumination of a truth, that there are absolute antinomies in politics and religion so fixed and final that it would be unnatural were they solved.

> Jean: Father, they aren't 'murderers.'
> Sergeant: What else are they then?
> Jean: They're patriots, soldiers. . . .
> Sergeant: Ah, nonsense, nonsense, they're common murderers.
> Jean: There's such a thing as a national soul, and there are political principles and a political conscience and men must fight for them or perish. And that's not common murder. (30)

Jean has not only the ingrained prejudice of her father to contend with but she has also to try to convince a bigoted mother:

Jean: Both you and father knew from the first I was going to Home Rule meetings and the Gaelic League, and learning to speak the Gaelic.

Mrs. Sheridan: We thought all that was just light-headed fancy—the sort of craze young innocents from the North pick up first time they're let loose in Dublin.

Jean: While they're still able to think for themselves about their own country—before they're blinkered and blinded by stupid religious bigotry and political prejudice. (38, 39)

Coulter writes dialogue for Jean's mother to make unwittingly a highly revealing statement about Ireland's troubles:

Mrs. Sheridan: You'll learn yet, Jean. There are some things so different that it wouldn't be right or natural for them even to try to come together.

Jean: Mother! I wonder is that the truth of it? The meaning of this [rioting] in Ireland. And of what's happening in the world—the Bolshies and Britain, for instance. I remember a professor telling us that even in pure reasoning there are certain. . . . antinomies, contradictions, that can't be resolved. Fixed, absolute, final antinomies.

Mrs. Sheridan: 'Antinomies' is far above me, Jean. But I've seen for myself, there's differences in politics and religion that's like oil and water.

Jean: Holy oil and Boyne water! Absolute antinomies in religion and politics. Alas, poor Ireland! Partition, fixed and final. Partition for ever and ever, amen! (45)

Coulter is interested solely in the human problem of divided families in Belfast, a problem found in his own political relations with his brothers there. He creates a well-constructed play with a growing suspense leading up to Patterson's rescue. There is no exaggeration, no final recourse to an unbelievable conclusion, no *deus ex machina* to untie the knot. Coulter never deviates from realism; the weaknesses in the play are the familiarity of the plot and the lack of depth in the characters. He has provided just enough characterization to give the audience rapport with the family, to offer that necessary interest in, and involvement with, their fate. It is like looking through a glass window at a family whose relationship has been explained to us. We would rather be inside the characters' minds and hearts. Perhaps it is this which prevents the play from becoming great. At the end of *The Drums Are Out* we still have not a sufficient knowledge of the individual characters to enable them to live on in our imaginations and memories, but we do have a greater understanding and sympathy with the people of Northern Ireland in their divisive, but intensely human, problems. In the final analysis, it is that which concerns Coulter and which made the play such an extraordinary success in Dublin. A review of *Drums* in the *Irish Tatler and Sketcher* for August, 1948, said of it: "it is a useful and timely reminder that the Belfast Orangeman is a real Irishman and very little different in his essential human qualities from his nationalist Dublin prototype . . . this play is a fine piece of anti-partition propaganda because it preaches indirectly that our fellow Irishmen in the North are the right sort . . . and . . . it would be well worth our while to get to understand them."

The play takes place on July 12, and, coincidentally it opened at the Abbey Theatre on July 12, Orangemen's Day. At the end of the first act the famous Lambeg drums, distantly heard, are becoming louder, ominously suggesting tragedy ahead. The contrast between the violence in the streets and Matt McCann's absorption in his pigeons is a poignant reminder of life going on in the middle of tragedy. His concern for his "wee blue tumbler" is symbolic of the family concern for Jean's unborn child. Jean says significantly, "Maybe another generation will resolve the contradictions of this one" (45). This is a sad remark for us who read the play some twenty-five years later in the light of the present continued violence in Northern Ireland. It would seem that Coulter's view that the problems are unresolvable is the more realistic one.

At the end of the play on opening night the upsurge of emotion brought a storm of applause from the packed audience in Dublin as the famous Irish actor, Jack McGowran, played the huge Lambeg drum festooned with orange lilies, in, of all places, the Abbey Theatre, Dublin—a remarkable sight! Today Coulter would hesitate permitting the play to be performed since sympathy for both IRA and police in Northern Ireland has deteriorated into distrust and outright hostility, even disgust.

In 1971 he wrote a new play, "God's Ulsterman," in which he seeks to find the source of the apparently unresolved violence in Northern Ireland and to present the contemporary picture as clearly as possible. It is a two play sequence, the first play being a short preface to the second. The first play, entitled "Dark Days of Ancient Hate," attempts to explore the roots of Northern Ireland's division in a drama set in Cromwell's time in the chancel of a small Catholic church in Drogheda. Coulter depicts the rather stereotyped characters of Cromwell and his men surrounding the church as Fathers

John and Michael are attempting to hide the Blessed Sacrament and sacred vessels. Not surprisingly the priests are discovered, and roughly drawn over mud and stones to be shot at the stake, while the woman who aided them is killed by the sword. Throughout this rather wooden historical preface, soldiers sing psalms and Cromwell mouths such pieties as, "I thank Thee, Lord, that Thou sustainest me in this, Thy service, giving me strength to execute Thy righteous judgments upon these barbarous priests."[9]

"Dark Days of Ancient Hate" is a reminder of the religious prejudices which lie deep in Ireland's history. Unfortunately the rather rigid characterization may dull audience sensitivity to an awareness of the deep-rooted causes of Northern Ireland's problems. The play is merely a commentary on today's unfortunate situation, painting a picture of the violence and bloodshed of Cromwell and his soldiers. The cruelty in it is inadmissible but one is apt to react by reflecting that it happened over three hundred years ago when people were rather primitive and uneducated. Immediately there follows the second play set in the 1970s and we find the identical cruelty, violence, and bloodshed in an educated and supposedly sophisticated society. The characters in "Dark Days" are not fully rounded men but their dialogue is passionate and deeply prejudiced, designed to horrify the audience with its simultaneous hatred of Catholics and praise of God.

The second play, "The Red Hand of Ulster," heard on CBC Radio, Toronto, on February 9, 1974, depicts Northern Ireland's present state of upheaval and violence. Little has changed since Cromwell's time, and it is in this unfortunate comparison that the play's greatest strength lies. "The Red Hand of Ulster" is concerned with an Ian Paisley type of character in the Reverend Andrew McNeagh, who would also remind one of Cromwell in his hatred, bigotry, and scandalous recourse to God to bless his destructive work of arousing the Protestants to fight the Catholics of Northern Ireland. Coulter introduces a daughter, Liz, a liberal university student, who rebels against her father's prejudiced ideas. She makes an interesting comparison with the character, Jean, in *The Drums Are Out*. Both girls are educated young women who deplore the bigotry of their parents. Both have the courage of their convictions, and both suffer in different ways for their independent stands against narrow prejudice and violence. Whereas Jean marries an IRA man, Liz attempts to lead a protest movement to change conditions and bring peace. Jean sees her wounded husband taken away by his companions to an unknown fate, while Liz is killed in the mad violence of a counter movement.

"The Red Hand of Ulster" contains some heightened, impassioned, declamatory speeches against fanaticism and religious bigotry. In this play Coulter has distilled his own inner lifelong rebellion against the senseless violence in Northern Ireland. He traces it back to Cromwell and creates a situation in this play whereby he has university students protest in a public demonstration against naming a new campus building "Cromwell House." The leader of the protest is the daughter of the fanatical religious Orangeman, Reverend Andrew McNeagh. Liz is a much more dominant, outspoken character than Jean in *The Drums Are Out*. She despises all that her father upholds. She sees clearly the ignorance that is at its roots. She proclaims her manifesto in these words:

Our gospel is social justice—spiritual grace through social justice in terms of houses, health, welfare for all men everywhere. Race, color, creed, all mankind alike. We're out to fight for that. And the first thing we've got to do before even a start is possible here in Ulster is to make this hideous, devilish, Protestant-Catholic thing be known for what it is—a killing spiritual sickness. An irrelevance. A road-block barring all roads ahead. We want to free ourselves from carrying on the terrible curse of Cromwell.[10]

The pace is fast-moving and, although it takes place in the living room of the McNeagh home, one can hear the mob, the violence, the ominous sound of the Lambeg drums off stage. Within the living room there is confrontation, argument, student preparations for protest, a television interview with Liz, a poor Catholic woman's plea for mercy, and, at the end, the student bearers of the tragic news of Liz's death. It is the scene of heightened dramatic action throughout the play. Liz's mother is a contrast to Jean's mother in *The Drums Are Out*. Liz says of her bigotry that she is even worse than her father. In a confrontation about the welfare of a helpless little Catholic woman who is being driven from her home by the Protestants, Liz and her mother take opposite sides:

Mrs. McNeagh: She's a Catholic and her presence in a Protestant Street, the only Catholic in a Protestant Street—can't you see it could only be a cause of trouble. Thorn in the flesh, festering.

Liz: Yes, festering. Festering! Festering! This wound that Cromwell left—festering.

Mrs. McNeagh: Cromwell! What's got into you! What's this harping on Cromwell?

Liz: The curse of Ireland. That's what Irishmen call him.

Mrs. McNeagh: That's what Catholic Irishmen call him.

Liz: With reason. A sadist. A savage. He stole their lands. Massacred thousands. Tried to drive them into the sea. 'To hell or Connaught'. (18)

Throughout the play the Reverend Andrew McNeagh's voice is the voice of Cromwell heard in "Dark Days of Ancient Hate," the same ideology, the same resonances, almost the same words. The historic evolution of these people in three hundred years of violent upheaval is clearly evident in "The Red Hand of Ulster." Coulter reveals the roots in Cromwell's mad fanaticism and cruelty which nourished and gave rise to the Protestants' spirit of bias and intolerance, resulting in the kind of periodic uprisings evidenced in *The Drums Are Out*. The dash and heroism of the IRA men is romanticized in that play, producing in the audience a feeling of sympathy and admiration for that nationalistic, patriotic, heroic group. The police force are also depicted as men of integrity and bravery. In the twenty-five years that have since elapsed, the people of Ireland have changed notably. Today they take a dim view of the IRA, which has developed into a body of unscrupulous terrorists. Similarly, the people have lost confidence in the police. Coulter hopes that a new group may arise in Northern Ireland—a group of university students, committed neither to Catholic nor Protestant, but to modern socialism as the cure for man's sociopolitical ills. It is this group that Coulter highlights in "The Red Hand of Ulster." Although the characters are not fully developed, the present feelings among the factions of Northern Ireland are strongly emphasized, and it is this that is Coulter's dramatic contribution. He has revealed the naked roots and permitted us to see the evolving hatreds based on rank ignorance and prejudice which seems to offer no hope for the future of Northern Ireland.

The Drums Are Out and "The Red Hand of Ulster," together with its companion piece, "Dark Days of Ancient Hate," represent Coulter's contribution to the people of Northern Ireland in their agony of blind suffering over a controversy that is totally meaningless to Coulter and the many other thinking people who share his balanced, unbiased views. These plays were not written in the same spirit as those propaganda plays, for example, which dramatists wrote during World War II, and which, because their partisan prejudices were stronger than their artistic purposes, were doomed to failure. Coulter wrote with a deep sense of love and commitment to Ireland—to both north and south—and with a genuine desire to use the theater as a mirror in which Catholic and Protestant alike might see the unreasonableness of their prejudices. These plays on Ireland's agony are his *ave et vale*, his hail and farewell. He has searched the sources and revealed the crises as seen in his own lifetime. Indeed, in all of his Ulster plays, from the early peasant drama, through the modern comedies, to the serious religious-political plays, Coulter has followed Yeats' advice to give the people a mirror in which every man could see his own image. Whether or not they will face up to that image is not for Coulter to predict.

With the conclusion of the early Ulster plays, Coulter, on his arrival in Canada, began seriously to study the possibilities of writing Canadian plays. Once again he used the principal talent at his disposal, his unique gift for the faithful reproduction of the nuances of speech and the ability to weave these into a poetic texture of language that would integrate atmosphere, dialogue, and character into a genuine tapestry or a living picture of his newly adopted country—Canada. Not surprisingly, his ear was not attuned to the unfamiliar sounds of Canadian speech, his artistry unable at first to cope with the vocabulary, the idioms, the slang, and the elisions. He worked unremittingly to acquire a knowledge of Canadian speech; and he was partially successful in producing a body of work that was certainly not of Ulster, though whether or not it was genuinely Canadian in tone and quality is a decision for the Canadian reader and theatergoer to decide.

CHAPTER 3

Riel *and the Canadian Plays*

WHEN John Coulter arrived in Canada in the summer of 1936, he found himself in a country where theater was prized but native English Canadian drama was at a premium. Not only had England, the United States, and France been variously influencing Canadian standards of theater for more than two centuries but they had also been supplying the actors and plays. Each Canadian city had its theaters where British, French, and American touring companies brought the best in non-Canadian fare. It is true that Canadian playwrights were actively engaged in writing plays but these were *radio* dramas—the only outlet for their talents. Because of Coulter's long association with BBC radio in Belfast and London, he turned naturally to CBC radio in Toronto. Some of his work had already been produced on CBC shortwave from London so that he was not entirely unknown. There he found an outlet for his artistic talents and for the next forty years he was a regular contributor to CBC radio and later on an occasional contributor to television.

In attempting to write Canadian plays Coulter found it necessary to frequent the corner drugstores, to listen to the chatter of young Canadians, and then go home to spend long hours trying painfully to reproduce what he had heard. After many unsuccessful efforts, he at last turned to something more fruitful—Canadian history. If he could not transpose the contemporary Canadian dialect on paper, he might at least seek some rapport with the Canadian spirit. It is significant that he found it in the one facet of Canadian history similar to "the troubles" of Northern Ireland, the rebellion of Louis Riel, which brought to the surface all the old hostilities between French and English, Catholic and Orangeman, Irish and Scot, Métis and the Canadian Government. French Canada's leaning toward what the Irish would call "partition," and its dissatisfaction with what Ulstermen would identify as "Home Rule," came significantly to light in the political battles that followed. With few exceptions, Coulter's Canadian plays emphasize that spirit of rebellion against injustice so familiar to the heart of an Irishman. Because he understood the passion beneath such agony, Coulter was successful, particularly with his trilogy, *Riel, The Crime of Louis Riel*, and *The Trial of Louis Riel*. In these plays he reawakens the spirit of that great leader in Manitoba, the half French, half Indian Métis, Riel. His other efforts deal likewise with the history of French Quebec in a group of radio plays: "A Tale of Old Quebec," "Quebec in 1670," and "François Bigot and the Fall of Quebec." Another radio play, "The Trial of Joseph Howe," was commissioned in 1942 by CBC radio to educate potential citizens of Canada on the history and spirit of Canadians.

I Riel

Coulter's most successful Canadian play is *Riel*, an historical drama about the enigmatic and controversial leader of rebellion and founding father of Manitoba. No figure in Canadian history has aroused more passionate emotions of hatred and love. It was John Coulter who discovered Riel's significance in the life of Canada, and who revealed his heroic dimensions as a national hero. In the program notes to its January, 1975, triumphant revival, after twenty-five years, at the National Arts Centre in Ottawa, Coulter says that *Riel* was the result of his search for a hero "who has been pivotal in a dangerous revolutionary crisis and turning point in Canadian history." Perhaps he had read what Louis Riel himself said in 1869 to a British reporter: "Tell them our great thought is to resist being made Irishmen of."[1] Although Manitoba's relationship to Canada never paralleled Ireland's unhappy alliance with England, the analogy could be made with French Canada. The figure of Louis Riel, a French Indian, had many similarities to the heroes of Ireland's history of rebellion and liberation. Again in the 1975 program notes Coulter referred to Riel as a "dark and haunting symbol nagging our political conscience . . . creating a mixture of wonder and indignation. I see in his uprisings . . . the early beginnings of movements all over the world in which an emerging people . . . insist on being left alone to mature." Coulter, having been present during the outbursts of political protest in Northern Ireland, was quick to recognize in the turbulent figure of Louis Riel the one who "rides the political conscience of the nation . . . and is manifestly on his way to becoming the tragic hero at the heart of the Canadian myth."[2] As a result of his intense research into this phase of Canadian history, he was able to give dramatic significance to an event that most Canadians wanted to forget and which few understood.

Riel was first performed on February 25, 1950, in an inauspicious premiere production by the New Play Society in the small basement theater of Toronto's Royal Ontario Museum with Mavor Moore in the role of Riel. The following year it was revised for CBC radio's "Wednesday Night" program, and produced on April 4 and May 9, 1951; ten years later, on April 23 and 30, 1961, it was shown on the television "GM Presents," with Bruno Gerussi as Riel. It was televised in Canada, Great Britain, the United States, and several European countries. In 1972 it was published by the Cromlech Press, Hamilton. Yet it was not offered the major production it deserved until January 13, 1975, when it was performed under the direction of Jean Gascon at the National Arts Centre, Ottawa; it featured the French Canadian actor, Albert Millaire, as Louis Riel, and included a huge cast drawn from both French and English Canadian theater. It was followed by a CBC radio interview of Coulter and a banquet honoring him at the University of Ottawa.

Carlyle's essay, "On Heroes and Hero Worship," showing the necessity of heroes if a country is to achieve nationality, is vindicated in the Louis Riel myth. Prior to Coulter's play, the Canadian people lacked a leader of heroic proportions. With the dramatic appearance of Louis Riel in the Coulter play there was generated a new pride in Canadian history. It was definitely one of the facets contributing to the growth of Canadian nationalism in the 1960s. Louis Riel was a decisive figure in Canadian history, the symbol of French-British struggle for control of Canada. Although the two Riel rebellions in 1869 and 1885 were the last crusades of the Métis to preserve their culture, their identity, and their rightful claim to their own land, the politicians used Riel to incite French-British hostilities. The Métis revered Riel as a prophet and many Canadians today see in him an heroic statesman, a victimized leader, the Father of Manitoba, and the symbol of those Indian, French, and English elements that constitute Canada's heritage.

The action takes place in the Northwest Territories during the period from 1869 to 1886. The Hudson's Bay Company had sold the Métis land to Canada, but Riel rightfully claimed that land in the Red River area (now Manitoba) for his Métis people, under the

British flag. Coulter researched diligently the history of the Riel rebellion for an authentic background for his play. He learned that the Canadian government in Ottawa, the military, and the clergy all disputed Riel's legitimate and constitutional claim.

At the end of the 1869 uprising, Riel is overthrown and sorrowfully retreats to Montana where he marries and settles down with his family, but is always visited, like Joan of Arc, by his "voices" encouraging him to return. This, Coulter found, was a natural ending to Part I of his play. Part II begins some years later when the Métis send a delegation to plead with Riel to lead a new uprising. He does so in 1885 and again defeated, is tried for treason and hanged. In the trial which achieved international publicity Coulter was able to recreate drama and dialogue of excellent theatrical quality. Riel's cause became the subject of a reawakening of all the old hostilities: French versus British, Irish versus Ulstermen and Scots, Orangemen versus Catholics. Coulter thoroughly understood this kind of rebellion and thus he gives it an authenticity that the average Canadian writer could not have achieved. Despite the sacrifice of Riel almost a century ago, the Métis in 1975 are still among the most neglected minority groups in Canada.

This play has been described variously as epic, myth, legend, pageant, documentary, and montage. As an epic, *Riel* does recount the deeds of an historical hero in a series of events expressed in elevated language; as myth, it is a kind of allegory of a prophet who symbolizes the larger and deeper passions and beliefs of a nation; as legend, it is a story of a half legendary character in Canada's past who has assumed larger-than-life proportions; as pageant, it is a procession of stylized events, rich in their final effect; as documentary, it is a true, factual account of history; as montage, it is a composite picture of heterogeneous elements produced through a rapid succession of scenes.

But more powerful than any of these is its close resemblance to Brecht's epic theater. A comparison between the two reveals a similarity of form, despite the different reasons for approaching this form. Coulter's talents for language and story, as well as the cumbersome historical material involved, led him naturally to this approach. Brecht deliberately chose to create a form that would destroy the illusion of reality in order to force his audience to criticize existing unjust social conditions, with the naive expectancy of their turning to Marxism for relief. Coulter instinctively used whatever seemed best to portray the many complex circumstances of Riel's life, and, choosing artistically, he unwittingly selected a form not unlike Brecht's epic theater. Yet he had not seen Brecht's plays; indeed he wrote *Riel* almost simultaneously with Brecht's *Mother Courage* and four years before *The Caucasian Chalk Circle*. Brecht was a communist and a rebel. Coulter is a socialist who grew up in the middle of rebels; and he chose a rebel for his major Canadian play. Brecht said that "human character must be understood as the totality of all social conditions."[3] Certainly Riel represents oppressed people everywhere.

In construction, characterization, and language Brecht and Coulter have strong similarities. Brecht believed in a loose construction in his plays; Coulter found that he needed a loose construction for *Riel* in order to deal adequately with thirty scenes. Brecht insisted on the treatment of characters as types or caricatures rather than as real individuals in order to maintain detachment and avoid empathy between audience and character; Coulter found it difficult to create realistic Canadian characters and his characters in *Riel* were conceived to represent political, religious, and racial elements who emerged necessarily as types, caricatures, and symbols. Brecht insisted on a highly concentrated poetic language and a poetic approach to history which he said "can be studied in the so-called panoramas at sideshows in fairs"[4]; Coulter's strength was in this type of elevated language and in spectacle. Brecht worked with Erwin Piscator whose stage made use of every new technique in order to turn the theater into a forum; Coulter worked with Jean Gascon and Robert Prevost in the 1975 revival of *Riel* using modern documentary techniques.

Brecht's theories on audience detachment, distancing, and on theater's sociological and historical impact also parallel Coulter's. Brecht wanted the audience to be detached in order to reflect critically on the social and moral implications of his plays; Coulter also intended that the audience reflect on injustice. Brecht preferred that theatergoers witness past historical events rather than present realistic ones in order to learn a lesson from the past through distancing the audience; Coulter deals with past history for similar reasons. Brecht uses epic theater to give the sociological background and encourage hindsight comments; in *Riel* the original photographs of the historical figures were flashed on a screen so that the audience would compare them with the live actors before them, thereby providing the sociological background as well as the distancing. Brecht omitted suspense by telling the audience future events and thus detaching them from the illusion of realism; the audience at *Riel* knows the history of Riel and thus the same effect is realized—detachment and criticism. Brecht claimed that the epic theater alone could present the complexities of the human condition; Coulter's experience with *Riel* vindicated this. Brecht's theater is a combination of lecture hall and circus and is thus able to vividly illustrate historical events; Coulter used a courtroom scene and spectacle when faced with the task of depicting history.

Brecht's refusal to create fixed unchanging characters, his insistence that plays not depend on logical climax but rather on a total effect, his use of music and sets to comment on rather than accompany a play—are all techniques used by Coulter in *Riel*. In Brecht's theater no attempt is made to create fixed characters, but his characters change with the exigencies of life; as he said in his *A Short Organum for the Theatre* (from which the following quotations are taken): "If we insure that our characters on the stage are moved by social impulses and that these differ according to the period, then we make it harder for our spectator to identify himself with them." Coulter's character, Riel, emerges from oppression and mistreatment. He changes with the changing social conditions of his life. Brecht's epic theater rejects plots built on logic; instead, his plays unfold in a number of individual scenes, thus building up a total effect rather than depending on climax; Coulter's *Riel* consists of thirty separate situations gradually building up the desired effect on the audience. In this connection Brecht has said: "The episodes must not succeed one another indistinguishably but must give us a chance to interpose our judgment." Riel's death occurs as the final episode in a long series of episodes rather than as a climax. In Brecht's epic theater the setting, music, and choreography are distinct from the play, contradicting rather than adding to the dialogue, commenting on it, revealing mistakes in it. He says: "Music does not accompany except in the form of comment." In *Riel* the ominous repetition of the song's refrain, "We'll hang him up the river with your yah, yah, yah" (Part I, scene 8) when Riel is seemingly victorious, contradicts that victory. Brecht frees his stage designer from the necessity of providing realistic backgrounds: "he no longer has to give the illusion of a room or a locality. . . . It is enough for him to give hints . . . of greater historical or social interest." Coulter needed to give his stage designer great flexibility in order to provide a symbolic background for thirty scenes. The distancing, so necessary for Brecht's theater, causes familiar things to appear unusual and gives birth to a new understanding of the human condition; in *Riel* the audience sees Canadian history in a new and revealing light.

The basic intention of both Brecht's and Coulter's theater is the transformation of the field of human relations through the interaction of characters. Brecht insisted that his actors not impersonate but narrate their characters' lives; Coulter's Riel causes his audience to see, not Riel, but a great actor playing Riel for them. For Brecht the inner life of the character is irrelevant except as it is expressed in external actions; no attempt is made by Coulter to penetrate into the inner life of Riel. We know him only by his spoken words and actions—again having the effect of distancing. Brecht's interest lies not in the study of human nature but in human relations. He said: "We need a type of theatre which not only releases the feelings, insights and impulses within the particular historical field of human relations in which the action takes place, but employs and encourages those thoughts and feelings which help transform the field itself." Brecht maintained that it is the story that is important: "Everything hangs on the story. It is the heart of the theatrical performance." This is true of all of Coulter's plays. He is concerned with the story, the history, the human conditions of a people,—with human relations rather than with the delineation of one character. The story or sequence of events provides the basis for further ideas and criticism. Just as the basic unit of Brecht's theater is the interaction of characters so is it in Coulter's plays. Brecht is concerned with the outward signs of their relationships with each other. Coulter's talents are ideally suited to this kind of theater, and since he chose it intuitively, without any recourse to Brecht, so much the better for his discerning creativity.

Brecht and Coulter were deeply concerned with dialogue—the proper use of language to enhance the self-expression of their characters. Brecht placed great emphasis on the kind of dialogue that would contain the appropriate *gest*—that whole range of outward signs of social relationships. He said of this: "The realm of attitudes adopted by the characters towards one another is what we call the realm of gest. Physical attitude, tone of voice, and facial expression are all determined by a social gest. . . ." Coulter used dialogue possibly without formally intending to make it a receptacle for gesture, intonation, or facial expression; yet, because language is his forte, he provided the appropriate declamatory speeches, divinely inspired words, and homely interchanges of social expressions, ·that gave the actors the means for what Brecht would call *gest*. Brecht's sentence constructions, his biblical parallelisms, his subtle rhythms and sudden changes of cadence invite comparison with Coulter's. Each scene of Brecht's sets the tone for the next scene, and Coulter also has developed this technique. Although Brecht has been unjustly criticized for apparently renouncing emotions, he gives high priority to those emotions relating to justice, freedom, and justified anger. These also are Coulter's priorities.

A comparison of Shen Te's confession to the judges in Brecht's play, *The Good Woman of Setzuan*, and Riel's defense before his judges, is startling in its resemblance. I take the liberty of changing Coulter's dialogue into a short rather than a long line format making it easier for the reader to compare with Brecht's line:

Shen Te:	Riel:
Your injunction	The day of my birth
To be good and yet to live	I was helpless,
Was a thunderbolt:	And my mother took care of me,
It has torn me in two	And I lived.
I can't tell how it was	Today
But to be good to others	Although I am a man,
And myself at the same time	I am as helpless before this court
I could not do it	In the Dominion of Canada,
Your world is not an easy one,	And in this world,
illustrious ones!	As I was helpless
When we extend our hand to a	On the knees of my mother,
beggar, he tears it off for us	The day of my birth.
When we help the lost, we are lost	The North-West also
ourselves	Is my mother.
And so	It is my mother country
Since not to eat is to die	And I am sure my mother country
Who can long refuse to be bad?	will not kill me. . . .
As I lay prostrate beneath the	Anymore than my mother did,
weight of good intentions	Forty years ago when I came into
Ruin stared me in the face	this world.

It was when I was unjust that I ate
    good meat
And hobnobbed with the mighty
Why?
Why are bad deeds rewarded?
Good ones punished?
I enjoyed giving
I truly wished to be the Angel of
    the Slums
But washed by a foster-mother in
    the waters of the gutter
I developed a sharp eye
The time came when pity was a
    thorn in my side
And, later, when kind words
    turned to ashes in my mouth
And anger took over
I became a wolf
Find me guilty, then, illustrious
    ones.[5]

Because
Even if I have my faults,
She is my mother
And will see that I am true,
And be full of love for me.
I believe I have a mission.
I say humbly that through the
    grace of God—
Who is in this box with me—
I am the Prophet of the New World.
First I worked to get free
    institutions for Manitoba.
Now—
Though I was exiled from Manitoba
    for my pains—
They have those institutions
And I am here,
Hounded,
Outlawed. . . .[6]

Although both Coulter and Brecht use a highly concentrated poetic language, it is a popular language, a down-to-earth ordinary language, and very realistic. There is in both dramatists a rejection of traditional form as they seek to emphasize the human condition in their plays.

The resemblance in these two defenses is unmistakable. First the biblical tone in both speeches has the unconscious effect on the hearer of Christ speaking. Both Shen Te and Riel are sacrificial lambs before their shearers, two innocents before a guilty court. The irony in both discourses is obvious. Shen Te argues that her devotion to an impossible ideal caused her failure. As we listen we admire her extreme generosity, for we know we would not have taken even the first steps. Riel argues that his devotion to his ideal will not fail, but we, the spectators, know he is wrong. We know how impossible is his ideal: he is a doomed man. There is more irony here. Shen Te and Riel have learned that they suffer for their good deeds; but while Shen Te expects no help, Riel still hopes that his mother country will not kill him. For both, real love is folly; it is the scandal of Christianity—the kind of love to which Shen Te and Riel have been called—and a stumbling block and foolishness for any human being; only a God or a prophet could respond to such mad vulnerability. Shen Te proclaims herself too poor "For your great godly deeds"; but Riel says gently, "I am the prophet." Shen Te's lover exploited her, yet she continues to love him; Riel's love (Manitoba or rather Canada) exiled him for his good deeds, yet he continues to trust her. Shen Te has learned her lesson; Riel has yet to learn his. Both speak in the tones of the wise man. Both are the speakers of parables. The mood is one of injustice, alienation, estrangement. As the audience we are merely observers. Mankind is the object of investigation, and we are left by both dramatists to work out the meaning. A literal interpretation would lead us to the conclusion that human goodness is impossible; an existential interpretation would point to the necessity of this mad virtue in a meaningless universe; a communistic interpretation would denounce capitalistic governments and suggest some recourse to common sense alternatives. Both Brecht and Coulter seem to be searching for an ideology that would replace capitalism. Brecht manifestly expects the answer to be Marxism. Coulter perhaps expects some form of socialism, some ideal society where men can live side by side without prejudice or injustice, where there is mutual trust and the freedom to live unexploited by one's neighbors. For both men the ideal remains impossible of realization in today's world.

The effect on an audience of a Brechtian play is like that of poetry—a kind of ecstatic contemplation and a new wisdom. Coulter's *Riel* leaves us with a similar experience. Brecht's good characters are usually defeated even as Louis Riel experiences defeat as he is led to the scaffold. It is interesting to note that the conditions of life which led Brecht to create a new form for the theater caused other artists living at the same time in distant places to adopt a similar form; for this form is the only one that will fit the exigencies of the life they are representing on stage. John Coulter is one of these. Without imitation, he found his way to Brech's type of theater for his play, *Riel*, and it is this form that has given his play the substance and solidity that makes its revival a triumph and a joy.

To *Riel* Coulter added two more plays, *The Trial of Louis Riel* and *The Crime of Louis Riel*. The Regina, Saskatchewan, Chamber of Commerce commissioned Coulter to write *The Trial of Louis Riel* for the Centennial Year and it was produced on June 14, 1967, in the ballroom of Saskatchewan House in a mock-up of the original courthouse in which the audience were the spectators at the trial, adding more realism to the play. So successful was it that it has since become an annual tourist attraction each summer in Regina. It was published by the Oberon Press in Ottawa in 1968. *The Crime of Louis Riel* was presented at the Dominion Drama Festival in London, Ontario, on April 5, 1967, and was awarded the regional prize for the best Canadian play. It was revised for CBC Radio "Tuesday Night" program and presented on December 10, 1968.

The Trial of Louis Riel is a documentary of the actual trial in which Coulter takes Riel's words and weaves them into a dramatic tapestry of his own. Coulter read the entire transcript of the trial and then created his own imaginative version, keeping religiously to the substance and spirit of Riel's words. The Canadian poet, John Colombo, also read the original text of the defense and adapted, for *The Marxist Quarterly*, "The Prisoner's Address," the speech giving Riel's defense. He sent John Coulter a copy of this with the inscription, (referring to Riel's own words beginning with "God is in this box with me.") "From John Colombo to John Coulter—see p. 48 for Riel's own words which are hardly as good as those you gave him."[7] Such a compliment is entirely justified when one compares the original speech with Coulter's dramatic version. When Jean Gascon directed the 1975 production of *Riel*, he added to that play portions of the dialogue from *The Trial of Louis Riel* even though the original play, *Riel*, contains its version of the trial. Nathan Cohen, the famous Toronto critic, had said in 1962 in referring to *Riel* as "this brave and mythic drama,"[8] that he had only one adverse criticism to make: "I found the scenes which deal with Riel's trial for high treason the least satisfactory." Had Nathan Cohen lived to read the new play, *The Trial of Louis Riel*, he would no doubt have been entirely satisfied with these scenes. Coulter describes it as "a factual documentary in which I omitted any imaginative interpretation and crammed what had transpired in four or five days of trial into two or three hours."[9] This is not wholly true, for Coulter did indeed produce an imaginative as well as realistic drama. *The Trial of Louis Riel* is three times the length of the three trial scenes in the original play, *Riel*. Also in the original play there are eleven characters in the trial scenes whereas in *The Trial of Louis Riel* there are twenty-eight characters and much more lively debates. The characters are not types or caricatures or symbols as in the original play but real men with whom the audience can empathize. This is manifestly a different type of play: it is not epic theater, but realism, and it demands a different response from the audience. Riel's defense is, in the original play, considerably shorter and more poetic than is the long naturalistic defense in *The Trial*. As good documentary and realistic drama it succeeds in affecting the audience in an emotional catharsis of pity and fear, rather than in the critical and thought-provoking response produced by the epic-theater version of *Riel*.

The Crime of Louis Riel was freely adapted from the epic drama, *Riel*, and the historical records. It was designed for either open stage or proscenium presentation. It consists of a continuous flow of scenes with the aid of no more than indicative properties, setting, and modern stage lighting. This play is put in motion by the "Actor" who plays the part of the crown prosecutor. After a long, dramatic prologue the play opens with the scene between the Priest and Riel. The additional character of Marie, a young friend and admirer of Riel's, adds a note of romance to the first part of the play. This new version is considerably simpler than the original play and easier for less experienced companies to perform. It has a much smaller cast and is generally less costly to produce. As Herbert Whittaker, in the *Globe and Mail*, pointed out, "The new version was done, according to Coulter, because the epic, panoramic scale seems to have been blocking productions inside and outside of Canada. The new version can be played by a cast of fourteen."[10] The actor who reads the prologue invites the audience to join the jury who try Louis Riel. Functioning much like the stage manager in Thornton Wilder's *Our Town*, he serves as a Greek chorus; in addition, by his presence he continually reminds the audience that this is, after all, only a play—lest the audience become too absorbed and lose its critical function. The two rebellions in the original drama are telescoped into one in this shorter version, which concentrates on the rebellions as the foredoomed resistance of a primitive people against a strong and powerful political group. It is native resistance against an aggressive, alien take-over. In this play Coulter omitted the imaginative and poetic material that gave the original play its epic quality, and focussed instead on the practical elements of good theater guaranteed to result in a short, easily acted, financially viable play; and in this he succeeded.

The *Riel* trilogy has been responsible for bringing John Coulter to the attention of the Canadian people. From the forgotten playwright he has emerged as the dean of Canadian playwrights and rightfully taken his place among the patriarchs of theater in Canada. More than this, the *Riel* trilogy is responsible for an intensive research into the history of Riel by scholars and statesmen. It has helped to

bridge the gap between French and English Canada; it has brought
before the immediate public eye the still unsolved problems of the
Indian and Métis; it has provided Canada with a national hero and a
pride in its past history. Gordon Alderson, in a tribute to Coulter at
the Arts and Letters Club, said of *Riel* that it is impossible to esti-
mate the impact *Riel* had upon the Canadian people, so powerful
and so subtle has it been. Merrill Denison called it the first Canadian play of genuine stature. *Riel* established Coulter as a Canadian
playwright; and he is now acknowledged as a Canadian contributor
to Canadian literature, and, as the dramatic discoverer of Louis
Riel, the initiator of what is euphemistically referred to as the Riel
industry. Many of the tensions plaguing Canadian society are mir-
rored in Riel who has become the champion of native rights and of
French identity.

   Coulter's interest in the French Canadian people caused him to
delve also into the history of Quebec and his research resulted in
three plays: "A Tale of Old Quebec," "Quebec in 1670," and "François Bigot and the Fall of Quebec." "A Tale of Old Quebec" was
commissioned originally by BBC radio in 1935, and sent by
shortwave to CBC Montreal, September 13, 1935, as a salute to the
founding of Quebec. The research done for this whetted Coulter's
curiosity and caused him to search further. In 1940 he wrote
"Quebec in 1670," a short play for CBS radio in New York, part of
"The Living History Series" that CBS had commissioned him to do.
In 1960 he was given a grant by Canada Council to write historical
plays. Among the plays he created was "François Bigot and the Fall
of Quebec," purchased in 1970 by CBC radio, Toronto, but as yet
unproduced. These three plays show Coulter's intense interest in,
and concern for, the dissenting party in Canada's confederation.

II *"A Tale of Old Quebec"*

   "A Tale of Old Quebec" was the first Canadian play Coulter wrote
in England. He was commissioned to do it and it became the introduction to the kind of historical drama that was to form the greater
part of his life's work. He refers to it in his memoirs:

At that time I was busy with a commission for the BBC which, had I known
it, initiated what was to be my principal work for the rest of my life. They
had commissioned me to write a play for short wave transmission to Canada,
as a BBC salute to the Quebec Day celebrations in 1930 on the tercentenary

of the founding of that province. . . . I thought that this and other stories of that era . . . when the future of North America was still at issue between the British and the French—especially the decade of corruption and splendor which was the tragicomical phenomenon of Quebec before it fell to Wolfe—have all the elements of a magnificent spectacular for film or stage, or broadcast series, TV or radio.[11]

It was revived by CBC, Montreal, in 1940. Because it was originally written as a radio play, "A Tale of Old Quebec" must be judged artistically from that standpoint. It opens with a narrator and the style throughout is poetic prose and verse. It is, in fact, the precursor of Coulter's later verse dramas. The narrator says in his opening address:

> The story of Quebec
> Is the story of a city upon a rock—
> The great rock in the great river.
> It is a story
> Older than recorded time.
> Legend began it.
> History maintains it—
> Four hundred years of history,
> Since that day in 1535. . . .
> When three strange craft came sailing up the mighty river. . . .[12]

The image of the rock is maintained throughout the play; the solidity of rock like the solidarity of the Quebec people, reminds one of St. Peter and the Church: ". . . thou art Peter, and upon this rock I will build my Church and the gates of hell shall not prevail against it." (Matt. 16). English Canada can hardly be equated with the gates of hell, but one can see the similarity of Quebec, the rock, and the French Canadian people. Coulter's use of the rock as archetypal image is found in the quotation at the culminating point of the play:

> The strife, the valour, of the long ago
> Feels at her heartstrings. Strong and tall and vast
> She lies, touched with the sunset's golden grace
> A wondrous softness on her gray old face.

The story records the exploration of Jacques Cartier and his three French vessels; the eventual arrival of the missionary priests, brothers, and nuns; the ships of war from New England; Frontenac striking the first blow in the 125-year struggle, crucial in the shaping of the destiny of Canada; the final victory of Wolfe over Montcalm; and the fate of New France merging with the future of England in a common destiny—Canada.

As an example of early radio drama, it fulfilled the needs for this type of artistic communication: few characters, brevity, the action completely verbalized, setting provided by the listener's imagination, the narrator kept apart from the main action, no delay in the action. The pattern of a radio poetry play emphasized simple language, quickly shifting scenes, allegory, and symbolism. "A Tale of Old Quebec" was a successful radio play and those who heard it in Canada said it would serve well as Coulter's advance notice when he made Canada his home.

III   "Quebec in 1670"

The short play, "Quebec in 1670" written for CBS radio in New York for "The Living History Series" dealt with the fascinating story of the first small group of young girls, suitable for officers' wives, sent from France to Quebec at the request of Governor Jean Baptiste Talon. Coulter's main characters are four officers who dispute over first choice in this short, light comedy. Talon settles the dispute by having them draw lots. When the ship arrives, they discover not four but fifteen girls on board. This causes a new uproar among the officers and girls until all is settled amicably and husbands found for each. Thus the sturdy race of French Canadians began and flourished. This type of play, similar to the early Ulster folk plays, was especially suited to Coulter's talents.

IV   "François Bigot and the Fall of Quebec"

"François Bigot and the Fall of Quebec," one of the last Canadian history plays written by Coulter, was completed in 1968 and purchased by CBC radio, Toronto. It has not as yet been produced although David Gardner wrote of it: "I found it a most thorough piece of writing, a very believable and ironic historical reconstruction. . . . I think it is a possible TV [production]. . . . I think because of the subject matter it would have most appeal in Quebec. . . . It certainly is a fascinating slice of Quebec tradition."[13] This play is about a corrupt rogue who was a protegé of Madame de Pompadour. François Bigot set up a replica of the Court of Versailles in Quebec before the fall of the city. Coulter used, to advantage, the stimulating plot of Bigot's creation of a Madame de Québec and his cheating of King Louis by amassing a fortune for himself. When Quebec fell, one of the terms of capitulation was Bigot's safe conduct back to France where he was arrested, tried, and condemned to death but escaped the death penalty. Although Bigot never appears in the play, his presence is felt subtly throughout. Coulter referred to it in his memoirs as "the social phenomenon in which during the ten years of the last intendancy—Bigot's— Quebec became the New Versailles rivalling Versailles in France in endless banquettings, balls, gaming on a prodigious scale, and memorable because of corruption by government officials on a scale equally prodigious and unmatched ever since, even in Quebec."[14]

This tragicomedy maintains a pattern of ironic counterpoint throughout the play. Eighteenth-century people are interviewed on a twentieth-century television talk show. The interrogator often uses expressions unknown to the French or the French Canadian of that day, such as "father figure," referring to Bigot, which obviously is strange to his mistress, Madam de Pompadour. She uses eighteenth-century similes, for example, "Is affection weighed out like molasses in a grocer's scale?[15] Love between the devious courtier and herself, compared to the oozy quality of molasses, is as repellant as the character of Bigot himself. Subtle innuendos, half-truths, and political hedging characterize the dialogue of Madame de Pompadour, the notorious mistress, confidante, and adviser to King Louis XV. The language of the other fifteen characters interviewed characterizes them. Montcalm reveals himself to be a cultured, highly intelligent, compassionate man of integrity, while Major General Wolfe, his foil, is psychologically unsound, erratic, cruel, taking unfair advantage of a corrupt situation. The priest, Father Dosquet, is merely a stock figure, but he is given some telling lines such as: "what is cynicism? What but the withering of compassion" (15). Each person is interrogated about Bigot, and the character of the man is thus gradually rounded out. The questioner not only asks leading questions but also supplies, by his remarks, necessary information about the characters and the scandalous history of Bigot's ten-year reign in Quebec. The questioner is responsible, as in any television interview, for maintaining a fast-moving pace, as, for example, in his interview of General Wolfe:

Questioner: You were in command, were you not, of the English forces at
the siege of Quebec?
Wolfe: True.
Questioner: You were selected for this command by whom?
Wolfe: Mr. Pitt, Prime Minister of England advising His Majesty.
Questioner: King George. . . .
Wolfe: The Second.
Questioner: His Majesty and Mr. Pitt had a high opinion of your ability?
Wolfe: Manifestly.
Questioner: There is a story that from your beginnings as a subaltern you
were difficult to get on with. That you were prickly, quirky, a loner.
Wolfe: I have never lacked enemies. Nor the stimulus of their envy.
Questioner: Some went so far, did they not, as to say you were mad?
Wolfe: True. Duke of Newcastle. He said it to His Majesty. Who replied
that if so he hoped I would bite some of his other generals.
Questioner: Did you?
Wolfe: If I did, my bite had remarkably little effect. (26)

Coulter's play, once again, is very much like the Brecht epic
theater. The television interview technique has the effect of distancing the audience and providing them with the objectivity necessary
to formulating critical opinions about the sensitive background of
France in Canada. The musical background is a mélange of French,
Canadian, and English national anthems, ballroom music, and jin-
goistic martial themes, thus offering further commentary on the
forces that divided Canada from the beginning. The set is simply a
modern interviewing dais in a circle of light such as one would see in
a television studio, with hints of history in the background—
photographs of historic French and British figures, maps, heraldic
bearings, and arms. Written before Arthur Miller's play, *After the
Fall*, it has certain resemblances in structure. The pivotal figure, the
interviewer, serves the triple purpose of questioner, commentator
as Greek chorus, and the one who detaches the audience from the
illusion of reality. The drama, in two parts, is very much like a court
scene with the interrogation of witnesses, a technique Coulter has
used with success in *The Trial of Louis Riel* and "The Trial of Joseph
Howe," as well as in portions of his other plays where interviews
and confrontations serve the same purpose; examples are the television interview of Liz in "The Red Hand of Ulster," the housekeeper's interrogation of the priest in "Father Brady's New Pig,"
and several other like scenes from plays not yet discussed in this

book. In the final analysis, "François Bigot and the Fall of Quebec" is a colorful representation of history unknown to many Canadians, serving the double purpose of entertainment and instruction, an easy mode of exposing the causes of "the troubles" beneath the Separatist Movement in Canada.

V "The Trial of Joseph Howe"

"The Trial of Joseph Howe," prepared for The Canadian Council of Education for Citizenship, in cooperation with CBC, was presented on radio on February 4, 1942, during World War II. Designed to remind Canadians that the freedom for which they were fighting was not won easily, this play's theme was, of course, freedom of the press. In a memo from Coulter found in the notes for "The Trial of Joseph Howe" to the members of the CCEC, he explains what he hopes to achieve in this radio play: "For the special purposes of the CCEC I must select from several methods of treatment the one which: (a) Exploits the entertainment technique of radio show business to the fullest extent consonant with truthful presentation of the historic fact. (b) Emplants in a context of contemporary reference the germinal ideas. . . . (c) Makes the thing come alive."

John Coulter was specially trained in radio drama at BBC in London and Belfast. His understanding of radio scripts is evidenced in the same notes for "The Trial of Joseph Howe" where he says that radio scripts are "hybrid—half musical score . . . the sound effects . . . integral and not merely illustrative or incidental . . . the change of pace . . . not lost." Change of pace is exemplified by the slow tempo of the scene between Mrs. Howe and Joseph as well as by the slow "ticktock" scene in which the jury are considering their verdict. The narrator opens the play with a description of "the corrupt administration of that day"—the magistrates of Nova Scotia—"who are trying to stop the mouth of Joseph Howe."[16] After this opening the narrator takes the audience back in time to the beginning of Howe's troubles as young editor and owner of a local newspaper in Halifax, *The Novascotian.* Coulter presents him and his young wife in the living room of their home, discussing the following morning's controversial newspaper item, a letter to the editor, signed by one of Howe's friends, containing explicit and true accusations against corrupt local public officials. The result will be a charge of criminal libel against Joseph Howe. In very realistic dialogue, Coulter reveals their willingness to risk this in order to support freedom of the press, the real issue at stake. The background voices of newsboys, Scots, and Irish, favoring Howe, is appealing to the listeners' imaginations; the declaration to prosecute on the part of the magistrates prepares the radio audience for the trial in which Joseph Howe prepares his own defense. Courtroom defenses are Coulter's specialty. This one, based on Howe's actual defense, is more dramatic in Coulter's words: "I hope to convince them that they, and not I, are the real criminals here; and I shall be mistaken if it does not prove the downfall of their imbecility—the grave of their corruption."

Coulter presents the prosecution as trying in every way to prove themselves right. Even Chief Justice Haliburton begs the jury to vote against Howe. The jury leave amid an uproar, and the clock ticks the ominous minutes away—an excellent early radio device while the narrator speaks, counting the passing minutes. Within short order the jury returns with the verdict—NOT GUILTY! In the general uproar of praise for Howe, he is carried home and a holiday for Nova Scotia proclaimed. His last words have that dramatic appeal indicative of a patriotic play: "Remember and teach your children to remember how freedom of the press was won for Nova Scotia and for Canada."

The Canadian plays of Coulter are entirely historical since he found his talent for writing a Canadian play within the context of Canadian history. At the same time, his contribution to Canadian drama is significant because it encompasses style as well as subject matter. Mavor Moore, John Colombo, James Reaney, and other notable Canadian writers have at various times all said that John Coulter's high degree of professional skill greatly influenced younger Canadian writers. The gradual development of Canadian drama from the 1930s to the climactic 1960s, when an incredible number of young Canadians were responsible for a proliferation of new plays and new theaters exclusively devoted to Canadian drama, may be said without exaggeration to stem from the fire Coulter and others sparked in those early years. Besides an expertise in theater and radio he also brought, through his historical plays, a measure of patriotism and involvement in things Canadian to the Canadian people.

CHAPTER 4

Oblomov *and Other Plays*

THE immigrant-exile image is symbolic of Coulter's life and work. It provided the inspiration for some of his Irish plays and it was the driving force behind his Canadian plays. When not torn between the positive need to recreate, if only on paper, the people and scenes of his native land, and the equally imperative urge to capture the moods and spirit of his adopted country, Coulter would allow himself the freedom of inspiration welling up from his own unique spirit as a man, sensitive to friendship, to qualities of leadership in others, to human nature behind the masks. It was during these rare interludes in his life that he conceived the inspiration for *Mr. Churchill of England* (1942), "Sketch for a Portrait" (1943), "Oblomov" (1946), "Laugh, Yorick, Laugh" (1956), and its sequel, "A Capful of Pennies" (1967).

I *"Sketch for a Portrait"*

Of these five plays the one that touches Coulter's own life most poignantly, since it involves the deepest friendship of his life, is "Sketch for a Portrait" and its longer version, "One Weekend in Spring." The tragedy of this short play is not alone the nature of his theme, not just the fact that it was never produced, but the one word written across the top of the manuscript in Coulter's handwriting—"abandoned!" Why did he abandon this play? Was it because he could not get a producer? There is no indication in the archives of any earnest endeavors to do so, as there is with his other plays. Was it because he had written this play to get something out of his system, a gnawing pain that an artist can relieve only by recourse to his art? Or was it because he had not been entirely honest in portraying the real characters involved? Certain it is that the play needs rewriting—if only because the facts of Coulter's private life reveal that the drama has only partially come to grips with the tragic circumstance of its composition.

The theme of the play, "Sketch for a Portrait," is the disintegration of a deep friendship through fear of an emotional entanglement threatening to destroy the freedom of the individuals involved. In the play the friends are two young women, but in the real life situation which inspired the play they were in fact two young men—John Coulter and the Irish painter, James Sleator. When asked why he chose to write women into the play Coulter answered: "Why I wrote women into the play? There were several reasons but the decisive one was the need to distance the action, so that the imaginative artistic process should be relatively unhampered by the chain-and-ball of the actual real." In his memoirs, Coulter has said that his friendship with Jimmy Sleator was not homosexual.[1] He also said that he had had one or two inspirations for plays with a homosexual theme but had been persuaded (in the 1940s) by professional theater men whom he trusted, not to pursue them because no management would produce such a play. Perhaps that is why he chose two women; yet their relationship bordered on a latent lesbianism of which neither was wholly aware. The sensitivity employed here is unusual but the play is not entirely satisfactory. Knowing its background in Coulter's own life the reader realizes how much more powerful a play he could have written, had he used two men.

John Coulter and James Sleator were close friends from their earliest days as students at the art college in Belfast. Coulter's memoirs refer explicitly to this deep involvement. They shared the same studio-apartments for years in Belfast, Dublin, and London. It was an ideal friendship because it was the inspiration for much of their work. Coulter sat for some of Sleator's most successful portraits and he wrote some highly sensitive criticism of Sleator's work. Sleator listened to Coulter's ideas for plays, encouraged him in his work, and offered advice and suggestions. Sleator, moreover, shared the sorrows as well as the joys of Coulter's life. The memoirs recall a night in Belfast when the two young men sat with Coulter's dying father, who lay on a mattress on the floor of the family dining room, until in the early morning the elderly Mr. Coulter, who had lapsed into a coma, had all but passed away. Their friendship dissolved in 1935, the year before Coulter's marriage. Again in the memoirs, he refers to it: "My long and close friendship with Jimmy Sleator—having degenerated from a trustful and mutually advantageous partnership into a bondage made intolerable by destructive jealousies and consequent fiercely acrimonious disputes—came to an end."

"Sketch for a Portrait" was written in Canada in the early 1940s. Its setting recreates those days when he and Sleator, after being fellow students at Belfast's School of Art, shared a studio-apartment together in Dublin, with periods spent in Sandy Cove near Dublin in Gogarty's and Joyce's Martello Tower. All of Coulter's free time was spent with Sleator, in the third floor studio of Dorcas House opposite the Gresham Hotel where the caretaker was a character like O'Casey's Juno. It was near the Abbey Theatre where Coulter soon became acquainted with playwrights and actors who were to make the Abbey famous. Hanging in the foyer of the Abbey Theatre is Sleator's portrait of Fred O'Donovan as Robert Emmett in Lennox Robinson's play; O'Donovan posed only for the face, Coulter for all the rest. It was while rooming with Sleator that Coulter began to write his first "Deirdre" play which he called *Conochar*.

The setting for "Sketch for a Portrait" is a painter's studio apartment. Laura Milsome, a portrait painter, is about thirty-five years old. Her young friend and roommate Valerie Whitney is an art student of about twenty. Laura, decidedly the better artist, is seriously engaged on a portrait of Val. James Sleator had done just that: painted a portrait of Coulter, who kept a description of it in his files evidently taken from a local Belfast newspaper, probably of the early 1920s. Coulter himself was the author of the article, now available in the Coulter Archives, entitled: "Some Portraits and Other Paintings by James S. Sleator, R. H. A." Coulter says:

The artistic event of the moment in Belfast is the show of Sleator's paintings in Rodman's Gallery. There are thirty of them [expressing] . . . the artist's subtle and sensitive personal vision. In the portrait of John Coulter (27) the lighting, the chiaroscuro was the thing. . . . Sleator is . . . a lyrical poet whose medium of expression happens to be paint.

The author and critic goes on to describe Sleator as an artist who knows when to lay the brush down and call it finished. He is delicately perceptive of Sleator's talent, pointing out his ability to know precise relations of tone to tone, color to color; the different qualities emphasized in different portraits: character, grace, pose, line, plastic rhythms, color in conjunction with character; his singular gift for handling strong, bright colors; the color design built up like a piece of music. Sleator was later to become a prominent painter and president of the Royal Hibernian Academy.

"Sketch for a Portrait" and its longer version, "One Weekend in Spring," stresses the relationship between the two young women in a dialogue that is sharply realistic and almost painfully poignant. Laura, the artist, like Sleator, is the possessive partner in this friendship. She is unaware of her dependency on Valerie and blind to the binding nature of her love for the younger woman. She is aware only of her happiness in Val's company and jealous of any rival. It is her vulnerability, her blindness to the reality of the situation, that makes Laura's character so poignant. Valerie is young, detached, eager to marry Len, not superficial but certainly not experienced enough to realize to the fullest the extent of the pain she is causing Laura. Coulter explores the relationship with the perception that only one who has had the same experience could achieve:

Val: I've been thinking about us, Lollie. I've had you rather on my mind all day.

Laura: Ah, darling, you're so quick to sense it when things are not going right for me. One of the reasons why I've loved having you here. If anything happened now to take you away . . . I really don't know what I should do.

Val: I wish you wouldn't think like that about me, Lollie. I don't rate that high. There's nothing special about me—nothing you wouldn't get from any other girl.

Laura: What an extraordinary thing to say!

Val: But I'm *sure* there are lots of other girls who'd be simply thrilled to have a chance of living here, like I've done. I mean—the studio. People being painted. Things going on. It's so different, so exciting. Any girl would love it and be everything to you that I've been.

Laura: Please don't keep on saying such things.

Val: But Lollie it's true.

Laura: How can you!

Val: How can I what?

Laura: How can you be so dumb!

Val: Really!

Laura: You don't seem to have even a suspicion that saying such things may—hurt.

Val: I'm sorry.

Laura: Other girls! What I might get from them! As if it were a question of some sort of bargain! Don't you see? It isn't a question of measured-out give-and-take. It's a question of something that has come to *exist*. Between two people. Not any two people—one behind the counter and the first who comes into the shop. Between two particular people, Val. You and me. It's something that of course can't conceivably be switched to somebody else as substitute. You can only treasure it or destroy it. Either can of course destroy it, and have freedom. But for the other—heartbreak. You do see what I'm talking about?

Val: You might be talking about love. (31)

Subconsciously Val has been aware for some time of Laura's feelings and what they indicated. What she does not understand is the depth of love nor the tragedy of its destruction. It is perhaps the only thing in life that, once rejected, can never be recovered in quite the same way again. Trust has been destroyed with it. Val's obtuseness is illuminating to Laura, revealing, as it does, the positive lack in the younger woman of the ability to understand the deep hurt she is causing. Such a flaw in Val's character serves to sharpen Laura's realization of how completely she had overestimated Val's qualities as a person.

Coulter has achieved an emotional impact in this play based on a universal experience—the possessive love of one individual for another, its betrayal, causing a fresh assessment of oneself and one's friend. The characters necessary to achieve this end are three—Laura, Val, and Val's boyfriend Leonard whose presence has triggered off the confrontation. Unfortunately in the longer version of this play, "One Weekend in Spring," Coulter introduces Laura's former boyfriend, Lennox Ross, and Leonard's mother. This shifts the emphasis from the Laura-Val relationship to the Laura-Lennox relationship with an incredible climax revealing Leonard's mother and Lennox as the parents of Leonard. This melodramatic switch changes the whole caliber and direction of the play. However, the shorter version, "Sketch for a Portrait," concentrates completely on the Laura-Val relationship. It is similar to act one of "One Weekend in Spring" but needs a more in-depth treatment. The play Coulter "abandoned" explores an emotional relationship with such grace, tact, and subtlety that the reader would like to see it rewritten—perfected, as only John Coulter knows how. Even more powerful would be the real life drama of the two friends, John Coulter and James Sleator.

II Oblomov

Ivan Goncharov, the Russian novelist, published his now famous novel, *Oblomov*, in 1858. This humorous and philosophical study of the "superfluous man" has since become a classic. Coulter read the first English translation (published in 1929) and said that he was immediately attracted to the philosophy of the antiactivist, Oblomov: "I felt challenged by the difficulty of making a *play*, on the theme of inaction. But it must not be hurried. Must not be concocted. It must wait, for however long, until as it were, Elie Oblomov came to me in person, to pose for his portrait" (letter, July 19, 1975). He therefore carried this book around with him for fifteen years. Then suddenly one fine morning as Coulter awoke, there, at the foot of his bed, was Eli Oblomov![2] Coulter leaped out of bed and set to work immediately, writing the play that was to bring him international recognition, but not Canadian acclaim. It was presented at the Arts and Letters Club from March 6 to 9, 1946, in its premiere production as a stage play; it was also produced by the Group Theatre, Belfast, revived at the Arts and Letters Club in 1959, and presented at the Talbot Theatre at the University of Western Ontario in the summer of 1967. Yet it was never given the major production it deserves. This has been Mr. Coulter's experience with so many of his plays—a brief run at a little playhouse and then a successful adaptation on radio and television. The radio adaptation was given its premiere performance by the BBC under Val Gielgud and Donald McWhinney in 1946 and soon became famous with international audiences. It was presented on radio in Europe, Asia, Africa, and Australia in 1954. CBC, Toronto's "Wednesday Night" program on November 19, 1961, finally produced it, long after the production had succeeded in the eastern hemisphere. Coulter revised it for television as "Mr. Oblomov" and it was produced on CBC's "Playdate," November 1, 1962. It was translated into French by Antoinette Sainsbury, wife of the writer Geoffrey Sainsbury, and into more than a dozen other languages including Arabic and Urdu.

In actual fact, "Oblomov" is not an adaptation but a derivation: Coulter does not present an exact conversion from novel to drama. Whereas the novel *Oblomov* emphasizes the psychological lethargy of a cultivated and creative Russian gentleman and the sociological factors in Russian society that have contributed to his disintegration, Coulter examines the philosophical and comical aspects of such a change as it impinges on the temper of Oblomov's friends and relatives. Coulter's plot is the calculated attempt by friends to bring Oblomov back to their "sane" way of living, with his eventual escape back into the apathy known today as "oblomovism."

Oblomov's philosophy of life is very attractive to John Coulter: it is this that caused him to treat the novel with such respect and determined his decision to use it as a theme for a play. The subtleties of Oblomov's doctrine are intriguing. V. S. Pritchett, in *The Living Novel*, mentions some of them, calling Oblomov a saint, ready for canonization:

In a world of planners he puts himself to sleep. In a world of action he discovers the poetry of procrastination. In a world of passion he discovers the delicacies of reluctance. And when we reject his passivity he bears our secret desire for it like a martyr. . . . After we read this book we do not hate idleness, escapism, daydreaming: we love Oblomov. We have discovered a man, a new man whose existence we had never suspected; a ludicrous Russian nobleman who, we realize, has dwelt for a long time not in Russia but in ourselves.[3]

Coulter is deeply interested in the man who is a nonconformist; who espouses art rather than a lucrative business; who spends his time in thought rather than in feverish activity; who is an unwilling exile, unable to shape events, yet giving prophetic voice to them. Originally a fusion of Hamlet and Don Quixote, he was first given a name, "the superfluous man," by Turgenev.[4] It was Goncharov who finally gave him to us fully and completely in Oblomov. The imagination quickly fastens on him because we see ourselves in him. The experience is universal. Robie Macauley in his article "The Superfluous Man" says of him: "More than ever before we are living in the time of The Superfluous Man. He is the grandchild of the hero, no longer believing that he can shape events but reluctant to surrender his human role and become a cog. He becomes an unwilling exile and his anguish is felt everywhere in our literature. We despise him and love him as we despise and love ourselves."[5] It is the contemporary man epitomized in, for example, Alexander Solzhenitzyn— the thinker, the articulator of contemporary man's ills. When Coulter chose Oblomov for the hero of his play, the symbolic representative of everyman, he was choosing wisely. It is understandable that the play had international coverage on radio; its neglect as a stage play in Canada reflects once again the fact that a writer is often not accepted first in his own country.

Coulter's play opens and closes with Oblomov in bed. There is something inherently comical in Oblomov's insistence on remaining in a horizontal position the better to think! Coulter cleverly introduces two visitors in the first act: a scoundrel, Tarantiev, and a friend, Stolz. Both, for different motives, are eager to get him out of bed; Tarantiev to move him into the widow Agafia's home, the better to exploit him; Stolz to introduce him to the beautiful Olga, in order to interest him in the world of activity once again. Stolz and Oblomov discuss work in a telling statement on the "illusion of purpose" in work:

> Oblomov: But when are you going to live?
> Stolz: Work is life for me.
> Oblomov: Work for work's sake?
> Stolz: Exactly.
> Oblomov: Come, come, you can't seriously mean that.
> Stolz: But indeed I do.
> Oblomov: But that's mere barbarism.
> Stolz: I don't think so. Work gives life *purpose*. And zest and meaning.
> Oblomov: Purpose?
> Stolz: Or at least the illusion of purpose, which surely is needed if we're to go on living.
> Oblomov: Is it—needed?[6]

Act II brings Stolz and Oblomov to Olga's elegant home. Oblomov makes the observation on the superficiality of the social life:

Even the youngest—whatever they do, it's false. Only a cloak to cover up the terrifying emptiness. The fatal disenchantment of knowing themselves completely out of touch with anything true and deep and real. If only they could muster up the courage and intelligence to leave their noisy self-deception and withdraw . . . trying to understand something of the mystery of their own being and so of life itself. (33)

In Act II, scene 2, Oblomov has fallen in love with Olga but fearful that such a relationship will fail, he falls back into apathy. Oblomov eventually marries his housekeeper and Olga marries Stolz. They all try to help but Oblomov refuses as he moves back into bed with these words to Stolz:

I know myself. And what I know myself to be, that I accept, in all humility. The ripe fruit falls, into the bosom of Mother Earth. It is nature's way. Here I am with Zakhar and Agafia. I have *chosen* this—grave—as you call it. Why try to drag me out? If you persist, my dear fellow, can't you see all you will do is tear me in pieces. (88)

The complex personality of Oblomov, with its seemingly dead calm of inertia, has been captured by Coulter in this seriocomic study. There is a quiet irony throughout the play in its social comedy. Oblomov's relations with his servant, Zakhar, from the opening scene of the play reveal not only the humor of the situation but also the protective attitude of the Russian servant toward his master. There is the comedy of vegetative boredom throughout, the comic-romantic possibilities of laziness, the caprice and mood of the love scenes—the combination of poetic and comic that Coulter has been able to maintain from beginning to end. The character of Stolz is an energetic foil for Oblomov: where he says "Yes" with alacrity to life's demands, Oblomov says dispassionately, "No"! Oblomov, the comic philosopher, a diverting eccentric, settles for comfortable squalor. The play is a tragicomedy, with fine humor in the early scenes gradually giving way to pathos in the end.

Nathan Cohen, the drama critic for the *Toronto Star*, reviewed Mr. Coulter's play in 1959 and pointed out the difficulties inherent in writing a play about inertia. If boredom overcomes the hero, Cohen contends, it is likely that it will also overcome the audience unless the playwright is ingenious enough to keep the audience awake. Cohen concedes that Coulter has written a play that is, "funny in spots, sad in others,"[7] but he asks, "what does the whole thing mean?" He suggests that we do not know "whether he is rationalizing his ennui, expounding a serious view, or is just ill and doesn't realize it." In 1948, in an article on Oblomov in *The Standard Magazine*, Coulter had described his theme as "the complete negation of action and the personification of conscious and deliberate withdrawal from a decadent civilization."[8] Cohen's second surmise is indeed the answer: through Oblomov, Coulter is expounding a serious view. The problem being dealt with here has plagued all men of thought who have been condemned for their apparent inactivity. Because Oblomov fails to produce a book, a play, even a short philosophical article, our society would judge him as either lazy or ill. Coulter would say that Oblomov has recognized the decadence of the society in which he is living and has consciously withdrawn from it, feeling that no contribution of his could possibly redeem it. This does come through loud and clear in the dialogue and inactivity of Oblomov. It is epitomized in his words to his friend, Stolz: "What was ambition for me? In spring, lobsters and oysters; ordering new clothes at a fashionable tailor's; calling on the best families; shaking hands with the Prince. That, and talking knowingly about painting, music, books—just to show that I *could* talk. Pah! Either I didn't understand the life about me, or it wasn't worth my thought. Perhaps I judged it to be worthless, quite" (23).

Oblomov describes life—the sort of life that his contemporaries are living—as "That sort of life—what's the point of it? A noisy wisp of nothingness whirling in a void. Listen to them now: gossiping, backbiting . . ."(33). This is a withdrawal into the philosophy of Sartre's existentialism—the meaninglessness of life; but where Sartre would advocate doing the best with it, Oblomov would simply follow it out to its logical conclusions—withdraw and do nothing. Olga describes him as being simple, innocent, guileless but with extraordinary subtlety. This combination of subtle intelligence and simplicity means that he is capable of clarity of vision and singlemindedness of purpose. He sees life as it is and he concludes that there is only one answer—withdrawal. There is no indication in the play that he is mentally ill or wantonly lazy—only that he is weary of a meaningless existence and answers it with inertia. The only thing that finally arouses him is his love for Olga. He says: "Oh, where have I been buried? Why, it's as if I'd emerged from a long winter passage, bleak and dark. And now, now the sap starts up again, up out of the bitter root. I walk in the blossoming spring and in my mind it is also spring" (47). But the image of the natural blossom, a metaphor for love, turns itself into the man-made image of hate as the firecracker bursts into an artificial flower of light in the sky and Oblomov regards the rocket stick which falls from it as "The withered stem of your lovely celestial flower" (49). This image, though it appears only once, is central to the meaning of Coulter's play. He has Oblomov answer Olga's reproof of his "talk about rocket-sticks falling and flowers withering" with "Forgive me, darling. Yet isn't it always so: at the top of joy the hint of grief." The audience is left with the uncomfortable realization that Coulter is not only referring to personal joys and sorrows but to the withered flowers of so-called "progress" in our technological age which has culminated in atomic warfare—the curse of contemporary society— that paradoxically has brought peace. Coulter wrote this play at the end of World War II. Oblomov's experience of life makes him doubt the possibility of long-lasting love with Olga. Rather than see it also wither, he prefers to leave Olga. He warns her not to speak of their love because when it is given verbal utterance the bloom will begin to fade. Later in the play, when it is autumn and he discovers that the gossipers are talking of their love and possible marriage, he says that the desolate autumn reminds him of his own leaves falling, a familiar nineteenth-century romantic phrase, indicating that love was not enough to keep him from the despair generated by this decadent civilization. At the end of the play snow is falling and Oblomov likens its cold whiteness to death. Stolz reprimands him because his outlook has not changed. Oblomov replies: "Why should it? I've found no new compelling reason to change. The part of wisdom, surely, is simply to accept" (85). Oblomov describes his position metaphorically: "The ripe fruit falls into the bosom of Mother Earth. It is nature's way." Alexander Pope expressed it this way in his "Essay on Man":

> Fixed like a plant on his peculiar spot,
> To draw nutrition, propagate and rot;
> Or, meteor-like, flame lawless thro' the void,
> Destroying others, by himself destroy'd.[9]

"Oblomov" is one of Coulter's finest efforts, but it has been almost totally neglected as a stage play. It has infinite possibilities, is in no way dated, and offers a challenge to any creative director. In *The Life of Acting*, Herbert Scott,[10] the renowned coach at London's Old Vic Theater, gives several pages to expounding dialogue from Coulter's "Oblomov" as test and training in subtleties of stage speech. Obviously "Oblomov" deserves at least a reading by Canadian stage directors and dramaturges.

III   *"Mr. Churchill of England"*

Coulter's sensitivity to the qualities of leadership led him to write the stage play, "Mr. Churchill of England." Produced in Toronto in 1942, it received favorable reviews and was revised for CBC radio the following year. In 1944 Coulter rewrote it as the biography *Churchill* which was published by the Ryerson Press, and it received favorable reviews from several literary critics.

In the original version, Coulter used the living newspaper technique, a flexible method in which description, dialogue, symbolism, and excerpts from Churchill's speeches are woven into a dramatic whole. A rapid, panoramic sketch, the play attempts to bring the essential facts into a series of vignettes, selected from the

most colorful episodes in the life of Churchill. The play is divided
into two parts consisting of a total of fourteen scenes. Part I consists
of nine scenes: The Races 1901, Constituency 1909, Gangsters 1911,
Old Guard 1912, Free Speech 1912, Forewarning 1912, Forearming
1912–14, Grand Fleet 1914, Crisis 1914. In Part II there are five
scenes: Polo 1921, Crash 1922, Respite 1924, England Awake!
1931–39, Front Line 1940.

Except for the small talk the dialogue is exactly what Churchill,
Admiral Jackie Fisher, and the cabinet ministers said, as derived
from their recorded speeches and opinions. Coulter gives the theme
of his play when he introduces it on radio: "Mr. Winston Churchill
stands in an almost symbolic relation to the story of British democracy in our time. . . . The whole thing was allowed to happen twice
over in a brief space of time. First in the years leading up to the
outbreak of war in 1914. And again in the years before September
1939. This singular and in a way alarming instance of history being
allowed to repeat itself through our befuddled negligence, provides
the structural frame on which the theme of the play develops."[11]
The radio play differs little from the original stage play except where
the art form of radio demands different techniques. Since it was
planned to be presented on four different evenings as a serial
documentary, it was therefore divided into four parts. Part I opens,
as in the stage play, with the races. It emphasizes young Churchill's
demand that the fleet be put in readiness for war. Part II stresses
Britain's ultimatum to Germany—that she will declare war if Germany does not stop its interference with Belgium. Part III opens
with the announcement that in 1914 Churchill had the British Navy
ready for war. This section ends with the Armistice and Churchill's
demand for rearmament in England as Germany becomes strong
before World War II. Part IV opens with the announcer giving the
background from 1931–1939, the terrible persecution of the Jewish
people by the Nazis, interspersed with actual speeches of Churchill
and Chamberlain, his election as Prime Minister and his visit to the
United States. It ends with an excerpt from Churchill's speech
avowing his hope that Britain and America will walk together in
justice and in peace.

This drama witnesses to the versatility of Coulter in its use of an
entirely new technique, the stage documentary, not yet used in
Canada. It had been created for the New York stage in the production of *One Third of the Nation* and had served admirably to instill

the excitement needed for such a play. Because of Coulter's long association with radio drama, he found it comparatively easy to incorporate radio techniques into his stage play in order to generate excitement in various scenes. He researched the subject thoroughly, examining old newspapers, chronologies, books on British politics, the family history of Churchill and his wife as far back as Gladstone, Disraeli, and Queen Victoria. Coulter's Ulster background and personality provided the spark of color and drama in the scenes of confrontation. As a Canadian immigrant, he adapted the tone to the spirit of North America, thus giving it a more universal quality. Coulter said of Churchill "that merely to record his story is to record the tragic tale of nations moving to war as if by some obscure compulsion inescapable as doom."[12]

The scenes in this fast-moving series include a newspaper office, a radio studio, a café, a London Street, a London crowd watching a spectacular air raid. Sound effects are dramatic in intensity: the noise of a newspaper press, a boy selling newspapers, bombs bursting, a marching regiment, a band on the street, the backstage voice of Churchill on microphone giving Parliamentary speeches, casual songs during the war being sung by the ordinary people. The play sheds a new light on this tory-liberal, this romantic-imperialist. The enemy of Nazism and champion of democracy is especially highlighted in the cabinet meeting on the eve of World War II—a scene of pure dramatic quality. As both a broadcaster and playwright, Coulter is particularly fitted to write such a documentary and "living newspaper" spectacle. Through dialogue and dramatic effects he makes us see Churchill—the boy, the son, the husband, the debater, the member of parliament, the writer, artist, soldier, strategist, and leader.

Only Churchill, his wife, and Admiral Jackie Fisher are actual portraits of real people. The rest of the cast are imaginary and represent a cross section of the British public. The play is a combination of biography, dramatic sketch, and impressionistic study. It serves to show, in a realistic way, the steady growth of Churchill from boyhood to international leadership. There is consistency in his behavior to uphold what he genuinely believes in: the changes in his choices are not changes in principle, for he refuses to compromise when integrity is at stake. All this is emphasized in Coulter's play. The dialogue consists of many famous bits of Churchill rhetoric, interspersed with Coulter's dry wit. Churchill is a man

Coulter understands; his stubborn courage to fight for his convictions in the face of every obstacle is a quality endearing to the Ulsterman. Indeed, he had long had heroic qualities for Coulter since, as a young man, Coulter had witnessed, from the third floor window of the William Moyes Textile Designing Business in Belfast, Churchill's courageous strategy to escape an angry Ulster mob who had gathered in front of the Grand Central Hotel to obstruct his passage to the meeting where he would address the Ulster Nationalists in favor of Home Rule. Rather than escape through a back door, Churchill preferred to walk out with his wife and in full view of the mob, bow pleasantly, wave his hat, as though they were his supporters, and coolly leave by car for the meeting before the crowd had gotten over their astonishment. Such a man was bound to become a great leader, an ideal subject for a successful play.

IV   "Laugh, Yorick, Laugh"

John Coulter's obsession with the men behind the masks began in those early days of his youth when he attended the Abbey Theatre in Dublin and gradually became acquainted with its outstanding actors and directors: Arthur Sinclair, Sydney Morgan, Barry Fitzgerald, Fred O'Donovan, Sara Allgood, and Maire O'Neill; and later, Micheal MacLiammoir, Hilton Edwards, Ria Mooney, Lennox Robinson, Jack Macgowran, and Brien Friel. This experience was repeated in London where he frequented London's West End theaters, and became acquainted with some of the great British directors and actors: J. B. Fagan, Laurence Olivier, Tyrone Guthrie, Michel Saint-Denis, George Devine, Alec Clunes, John Fernald, Donald Wolfit, and Sir Cedric Hardwick; Sybil Thorndike, Edith Evans, Flora Robson, Irene Worth, Renee Asherson, Barbara Couper, Moirs Lister, Marie Ney, Mary Ellis, and Susan Hampshire. It is not surprising then, that he would one day be inspired to write a play about players; what was unusual was the fact that, having written and completed "Laugh, Yorick, Laugh," he should be astounded at being accused by his friends of having written a stage portrait of Laurence Olivier and his wife, Vivien Leigh! Any objective reader would indeed see Laurence Olivier in the title role, but not of course Vivien Leigh, whose excellent acting was far superior to the superficial character and limited talents of the young woman actress who lives with and is unfaithful to the main character. However, the character Stephen Bentham is so powerfully like

Laurence Olivier that Coulter was advised to abandon the play because no producer would accept it at that time. Written in England in 1956, it has never been produced and remains in the Coulter Archives at McMaster University, Mills Memorial Library, in Hamilton, Ontario. It is a play in the traditional style of realism with enough melodrama to give it that zest necessary for a successful production of a play of its type. The dialogue is lively and the denouement completely unexpected.

"Laugh, Yorick, Laugh" is a tragicomedy of manners about two actors who live together, Stephen Bentham and Dulcie Graham. Stephen is a great Shakespearean actor and one of the best directors of the time. Dulcie is merely a television personality of limited talent. Coulter studies the impact of these two actors on each others' personalities in a drama that depicts Stephen attempting to reveal Dulcie's inept acting abilities only to be foiled at the end by the overwhelming support of her television audience. She leaves Stephen and he senses a great feeling of relief.

"Laugh, Yorick, Laugh" has the qualities of tragicomedy which is an impure art, partaking as it does of the nature of comedy and tragedy. Yet it manages to combine these two genres and to reconcile them. Interestingly, it is in the moments of comedy that the characters are defined. We see Stephen and Dulcie clearly in moments of comic confrontation. Yorick laughs at them; we laugh, but we carry away with us the picture of a disillusioned actor. Coulter says of this play:

I tried to portray a mood of destructive disillusion which I had noticed in actors who, having discovered their power and talent, and had success, discovered also a formula for success and were unwittingly betrayed by it—betrayed into loss of that artistic problem which is essential to all creative work. For actors this is the problem of interpretation which should present a challenge with each new role—a stimulus and 'fascination of what's difficult', the successful solution of which is artistic renewal and joy. In my play such an actor—in reaction to ecstatic applause for a bravura performance which his artistic conscience rejects as formula, a fake, a fraud, is suddenly overwhelmed by that mood of disillusion. . . . Who am I? What am I? . . . This curse the gods laid on me! Compulsive need to act![13]

Coulter's friends and artistic directors, Murray MacDonald, Michel Saint-Denis and George Devine, all told him they recognized this tragic figure as Laurence Olivier, although Coulter had not consciously written him into the role. In Stephen Bentham Coulter had succeeded in creating the great actor in that mood of destructive disillusion, with the superficial actress, Dulcie Graham, as a foil, drawing out all the complex characteristics of the successful actor who is surfeited with applause. It is an interesting study and entirely credible. Combined with this is the picture of the actor who has played a role so long (in this case, Hamlet) that the weaknesses of the character have crept into the very soul of the actor so that in private life he begins to give evidence of similar psychological strains. Only a new play and a new lease on life will free him from such bondage. The opportunity comes at the end of the play and the audience is left with the feeling that Stephen has been released.

This play is worthy of production. The characters are drawn with some subtlety; the dialogue is crisp and witty; the action moves swiftly to a climax; the scenes have enough variation to add zest; the cast totals only eight actors and is easily and inexpensively produceable, and the play is not dated. As in some of Coulter's other plays, the seasons symbolize the mood, so in this the bitter winter of Stephen's discontent is followed swiftly by a spring promising new life to the actor. The skull of Yorick sitting on Stephen's desk is also symbolic of the masks, the tragicomic mood that pervades this play. Hamlet's words to Yorick, as in disillusion he held the skull in his hands at the opening of the play, are applicable to Stephen: "A fellow of infinite jest, of most excellent fancy. . . . Where be your gibes now? your gambols? your songs? your flashes of merriment? . . . Not one now, to mock your own grinning? quite chapfallen?"[14] Stephen resembles the dead fool; he lacks the energy and the wit to rise above his disillusioned mood. Yorick is referred to in key scenes throughout the play. In the opening, when his offer to Sara of the Cleopatra role is refused and he recognizes the ennui in himself, he says: "All to what purpose? To what purpose, eh Yorick? Silence. The ultimate answer. Yet we keep on *asking*. Why? Why? What for? Been doing it since Adam probably, who screamed it out after he ate the apple. Prompted by a pain in his intellectual guts. Man, masochistic man. Success."[15] As he examines his present performance in *Othello* he sees the fool he is: "Knave and cheat and weak-willed acquiescent fool. . . . An actor on stage stagnating. Lacking the will to *act*. Conniving in sabotage of himself" (41). At the end when Sara has accepted the role of Cleopatra, Stephen turns to the skull of Yorick, takes the spring flowers and places them in the apertures of the skull saying: "Hey, Yorick! Spring again, Yorick! . . . Flowers, Yorick! Flowers by request! Let's wear our rue with a difference, shall we? 'Of all Christian souls I pray God!' God-a-mercy! Laugh, Yorick, Laugh!" (44).

V *"A Capful of Pennies"*

Coulter's decision to abandon "Yorick," because of its alleged resemblance to Laurence Olivier, did not mean that he would abandon the idea. Ten years later he took up the theme again and this time he chose to write the life of an actor long since dead—the great Edmund Kean. Coulter was well aware of Kean's association with theater in Canada. He knew that Edmund Kean had come to Canada in 1826, had acted in Shakespearean drama in Montreal and Quebec, had been hailed by Canadian theatergoers as the greatest living actor at a public banquet in recognition of his distinguished theatrical career, and had been paid the supreme compliment by the Huron Indians by being made a chief. All this fired Coulter's imagination. The play, originally entitled *This Glittering Dust*, was given its first production at the Central Library Theatre in Toronto on March 22, 1967, under the title "A Capful of Pennies." Brian Doherty said of it, "The part of Kean is an actor's dream."[16]

"A Capful of Pennies" is a play in three acts, a tragicomedy and portrait of Edmund Kean. Kean's life was in itself so melodramatic that the play seems unreal although factually faithful to it. His inability to separate reality from illusion, and the love-hate relationship he had with the audiences of London's West End theaters, as well as his failure to understand the nature of the magnetic appeal he had for women, make this play a rather complex drama.

It is the story of England's most legendary actor evoking the romantic period of British theater when the successful actor was the public's idol and pawn. Kean's genius was destroyed when he failed to respond to the public's conservative moral values. The theme of megalomania runs through Kean's life; it is this which fascinated Coulter, as indeed it did in the life of Louis Riel. All this is extremely difficult to contain in one play. We do not see Kean acting his great roles since his kind of acting would seem ludicrous today, but we see him instead in his private life. Coulter tries to tell it all in three acts of eleven scenes, compressing his material into a period of twelve months. It is not a success because there is just too much in the play to handle artistically.

Only the characters of Edmund Kean and Charlotte Cox are fairly
rounded personalities. The others are mere types. Kean comes
through as a passionate, violent megalomaniac, the subject of frequent emotional outbursts, impatient with social protocol, easily
moved by flatterers, given to heavy drinking, and most at home in
the slums. Charlotte Cox is a wealthy, superficial socialite, living by
a double standard, something of a nymphomaniac, passionately in-
fatuated with Kean. Coulter has not taken enough pains to show the
gradual development of their love, with the result that the audience
is puzzled by her sudden change at the end of the play into a
selfless, deeply loving woman. The rest of the cast are merely
background figures: Mary, Kean's wife, an ineffectual woman, un-
equal to his genius, unsuccessfully aspiring to dramatic as well as
social heights; Lee and Arnold, the managers of the Dorchester and
Drury Lane Theatres, simply voices imploring Kean to mend his
ways; Alderman Cox, Charlotte's cuckolded husband; Ann Carey,
Kean's slovenly, dissipated mother from the London slums;
Ophelia, his prostitute mistress; the Prince-Regent, and other
characters—fashionable men and women, ex-actors, butlers, members of the Drury Lane audiences.

Kean's dialogue is melodramatic and frequently interspersed with
quotations from Shakespeare. The language is pretentious but one
must remember the character of the actor who uttered such words
as those addressed to his wife in their last confrontation: "I had my
pick! Lascivious dolls! My harem of titled whores! I shall set up shop
with them! New idea in high-class bawdry! Kean's brothel of
duchesses!"[17] The action moves swiftly through many scenes of confrontation between Kean and his wife, his mistresses, and his managers. They serve to reveal his character and the agony of his efforts
to rise to the top of his profession only to destroy himself. One such
scene, a favorite of Tyrone Guthrie's who considered it one of the
most effective, is initiated by the remonstrances of Kean's Manager,
Mr. Arnold, of Drury Lane Theatre:

Arnold: Be wary, then! Be wary! You may take success too much for
granted. Perhaps it has come too easily of late?
Kean: Easily? Easily? I never knew you for a jester, sir. But that "easily"
is a master jest! Worthy Grimaldi's cap and bells! Shall I go fetch you the
cap and bells? I have bought success with anguish and blood. It has cost me
half my life. I shall die young. I feel death already in my bones and blood.
Its first small cloud floats up in my brain. Easily! Good heavens, what comic

irony! Oh what a comic gift you're hiding—under a bushel of dull horse sense!

Arnold: My dull horse sense tells me that cloud in your brain may well be brandy. Too much brandy—and too many nights misspent carousing and sleeping in any bed but your own and Mary's! (53)

In Kean, as in Stephen Bentham of "Laugh, Yorick, Laugh," Coulter has created his archetype of the actor—the man of tempestuous brilliance, vulnerable, impatient, idealistic, whose real life is the life of the stage, impinging to such a degree on his personal life that he unconsciously assumes the characteristics of the role he is playing; as a consequence, his own personality becomes submerged in that of the master actor. To such a one, every turn of fate becomes an opportunity to act a role rather than to react as a man, and, in so doing, to destroy himself. Jean-Paul Sartre, in his play on Kean, achieved this more economically and more artistically by ignoring the facts of Kean's life and dwelling instead on an exploration of the real versus the role-playing man. Because Kean ignored or blinded himself to reality, it is perhaps the playwright's prerogative to dissociate Kean from the factual and place him in the imaginative realm where indeed Kean, himself, dwelt with more ease. In the Canadian historical plays, particularly *Riel*, Coulter was able to place his characters factually in their true historical context, but these were men who faced reality and lived with the real. Coulter was not as successful with Kean whose factual life no audience could accept as credible.

CHAPTER 5

Radio and Television Adaptations
of the Plays

ROBERT Weaver, the director and producer of CBC radio drama in Toronto, and a longtime friend of John Coulter's, said of Coulter that his first love was the live stage. Although Coulter's success lay principally in his radio drama and eventually in a few television plays, these were always adaptations of original stage plays. Other than the two operas which CBC radio had commissioned, and which indeed had been written and shaped so that they could be easily adapted for television and the stage, almost all of Coulter's plays were first created for a live stage performance, and then adapted for radio and eventually for television. What he says of *Transit Through Fire* could be said in reverse of all his other plays: "We took pains to shape this work so that, after radio, it could be readily adapted for television, or—our ultimate goal—the stage."[1]

Both Herman Voaden, the Canadian dramatist[2], and Robert Weaver[3] have stated that Coulter came to Canada too soon and that he was born ahead of his time as far as Canadian drama was concerned: Voaden wrote, "If only Coulter had come in 1956 instead of 1936," while Weaver noted that "He came to Canada in his forties and he came twenty years too soon." They were referring to Canadian live theater which only made progress in a professional manner in the 1960s. Before that, most Canadian dramatists wrote for CBC radio. A new group of young writers initiated CBC television drama because the radio writers were prevented from doing so by CBC radio contract stipulations which forbade them to write for both CBC radio and CBC television.[4] They had to make their choice and since some of the older writers were afraid to risk their future on a new form of drama with which they might not be able to cope, they therefore decided to remain with radio.

As a result John Coulter, a freelance writer, was one of the few Canadian dramatists writing simultaneously for stage, radio, and television. Almost every one of his plays has three scripts, for live stage, radio, and television. The libretto written by Coulter for the opera *Deirdre* had its early origins in a stage play *Conochar* (1917), later revised for BBC radio as "Conochar's Queen" (1934). Another early stage play, "The Folks on Brickfield Street," was revised for BBC radio and retitled by them *Family Portrait* (1935); in 1956 it was adapted for television by Rita Greer Allan as "The Sponger." Still another stage play, "Holy Manhattan" (written in 1940), was revised for radio and produced on CBC "Theatre of Freedom" as "This Is My Country"; in 1955 it was adapted for television under the title "Come Back to Erin." The opera *Transit Through Fire*, composed in 1942 originally for radio, was adapted for concert stage in 1943 and finally for television in 1955. "Oblomov" was created for the stage in 1946, and later in the same year adapted for radio where it achieved international success; eventually, in 1962, it was revised for television and presented on the CBC television series "Playdate" as "Mr. Oblomov." *The Drums Are Out*, which had a highly success- ful presentation at the Abbey Theatre, Dublin, was revised for radio in 1950 and for television's "FM Theatre" in 1969. Coulter's most distinguished work, *Riel*, was written originally for stage in 1950, revised for radio in 1951, and for television's "GM Presents" in 1961. "Green Lawns and Peacocks" has gone through several revi- sions, for stage, radio, and television, under the title "While I Live"; but it failed to receive attention. All of Coulter's remaining plays have gone through at least two revisions for stage and radio.

I *Radio Drama*

Although it is true that theater was Coulter's first and only real love, he worked with radio from its beginnings and continued to do so over the long span of his life. His first produced play was an adaptation for BBC radio of a stage play "Sally's Chance" (1925) and his most recently completed stage play, "The Red Hand of Ulster," was revised for CBC radio and produced in 1974. He thoroughly understands the art form of radio drama. Indeed one of his most successful essays was that entitled *Radio Drama Is Not Theatre*, which was published by Macmillan in 1937. Originally a radio dialogue between Coulter and the actor Ivor Lewis, it had to be revised for publication in order, as Coulter says in the introduction, "to give the illusion of being spoken." The fact that Coulter would not allow it to be published in its original form as a radio script shows his sensitivity to the distinct techniques required for different media. In this essay Coulter describes the methods needed to produce artistic radio drama. He speaks of the voice as the single instrument which must take the place of the actors, their gestures, facial expressions, lighting, scenery. He calls for dialogue that seems simple, spontaneous, and natural. The radio dramatist has only the living voice and the sound effects with which to work. Coulter suggests that there be few characters—no more than six—whose voices vary sufficiently to be easily distinguished by the hearers. He asks for brevity—no long-winded speeches nor long drawn-out scenes. Musical interludes and frequent changes of scene are advisable. Because the voice establishes character—carrying conviction, emotion, etc.—it must not sound theatrically "trained" but must appear natural as the microphone isolates the sound of the voice and picks up every nuance. Coulter tells his readers to aim at simplicity with variety, avoiding all complications of plot, scene, sound, and language. He considered the best plays for radio to be those of well-reasoned argument, important themes, imaginative prose and verse, particularly about "country folk because their speech is still so full of savour—the direct expression of feeling and character."[5]

Coulter wrote this essay in 1937 when radio drama in Canada was still comparatively young. Much of what he said then is still applicable today; in fact, the most successful radio producers of drama at the present time have not added substantially to Coulter's original thesis. What they have added, Coulter has already observed in his radio dramas. For example, Felix Felton wrote in 1949, "It is in the creative act of the listener's imagination that the play ultimately achieves life."[6] He called for action that is completely verbalized; the sound effects must be first established in the dialogue. A narrator is necessary. The radio play, he said, is ideally suited for character study and fantasy, for history, folk heroes, romance, and psychology, for the detective thriller and suspense. In 1957, Abbot and Rider wrote *The Handbook of Broadcasting* in which they emphasized the importance of strong beginnings in radio drama to capture audience interest, set the theme, establish the characters. They deplored the fact that, "few noted writers for the stage have been attracted to radio . . . the radio drama has not yet been considered a serious literary form."[7] In 1974, Don Mowatt, director

and producer of CBC radio drama in Vancouver, added some perceptive comments to current ideas on radio plays. He said that they
must be highly condensed, much more than television or stage; the
use of stream-of-consciousness is perfect for radio; the elements of a
story or idea must be pieced together as in a mosaic; the radio play
has to be complete because it is not affected in its progress as in a
live stage play by audience reaction; the mind of one character talks
to the mind of another while they are saying something else, which
is easier to do on radio than on stage because the nuances of voice
are so pronounced, and past, present, and future relationships are
easily juxtaposed. "You can't portray walking," says Don Mowatt,
"so you avoid areas that deal with physical movement. That's why
you have to go into the mind—a mathematics of the mind rather
than a spatial conception."[8]

Coulter's radio drama varies considerably from his stage play as
he introduces narrators and changes dialogue to add more imaginative appeal and verbalize the action. He uses the radio media for
plays dealing with history, folk tales, suspense, and romance. He
invariably changes the opening of his radio play revisions in order to
strengthen the beginning of the play and thus immediately capture
the attention of his radio audience, establish the characters, and
clarify the theme. Coulter also condenses his plays considerably as
he revises them for radio. He makes more use of the soliloquy and
strives to achieve a psychological effect as mind speaks to mind. He
is aware of the importance of nuances in voices on radio and gives
directions accordingly.

II *Television Drama*

Television drama is an entirely different media and must be dealt
with on its own terms. Nathan Cohen said of television writers,
"How important it is to think not only in strictly visual terms, but in
TV visual terms which is an altogether different thing."[9] Don
Eccleston, director and producer for CBC-TV drama, Vancouver,
remarked, "In television, the images take the place of dialogue. In
television drama, there should be less dialogue and more movement
of characters."[10] Coulter cut his dialogue considerably and introduced much more movement in his television play revisions. "To
change a stage play into a television play one must sharpen it,
deepen it, express it in incredibly beautiful shots of actors in mean-
ingful relations," says Eccleston. "One must seek the substance,

quality and delineation of character in the detail of structure. One must be a good dramatist to write for television." Coulter's television dramas were successful because he reworked his script to allow for and enhance the pictorial element. He permitted the viewer to see life before hearing it. Coulter revealed character through incident. "The closest thing you can do with an image in a film is to make a line of poetry out of it. The juxtaposing of images creates another dimension," said Eccleston.

Having examined the different requirements for good radio and television drama, it will be interesting to note the changes made by John Coulter as he revised his stage play from live theater to radio to television. The two plays, "Oblomov" and *Riel*, are excellent examples of his technique and mastery of the different media.

III   *"Oblomov"*

"Oblomov" was initially produced as a stage play in a modest amateur production in 1946 at The Arts and Letters Club in Toronto and revived there in 1959. Its quality as a live stage play was obscured by the limitations of the production. Noted Canadian critics disagreed as to the merits of the play. Nathan Cohen felt that Coulter failed to establish the real cause of Oblomov's fate and the director did not clarify it. "He [the director] fails to clarify and impose his own definition of the meaning of things on which Mr. Coulter is vague."[11] Cohen also contended that you cannot dramatize apathy without causing the audience to feel apathetic. A surely unwarranted assumption! Mavor Moore argued that the role of Oblomov requires a virtuoso performance—success depends on one big star, rather than on producer or company. Also he says, "the play itself is the kind of gentle, warm tragicomedy that could only become a box-office success by virtue of an acting tour-de-force."[12] These two factors make a successful stage production difficult, whereas says Moore, "on radio . . . 'Oblomov' should be universally viable." Herbert Whittaker complimented Coulter's work. He said, "It is difficult to put a figure of inertia on a stage, which cries out for action, but Mr. Coulter holds the balance well by concentrating on the near rescue of Oblomov."[13]

The stage play is written in three acts for three sets, the living room of Oblomov's lodgings in Petersburg, the drawing room of Olga Ilynski's estate, and the squalid bedroom of Oblomov's final poverty-stricken tenement. Similarly there is a threefold change in form, from comedy in the first act, to romance in the second, to tragedy in the third. On live stage this pattern—which is inevitable, given the character of Oblomov—can also be frustrating to an audience prepared to see either comedy, or tragedy, or romance, but not all three. Unfortunately, "Oblomov" has never been given a major production on stage, so that one cannot fairly assess it. As a piece of literature it reads well, but Coulter leaves the character of Oblomov to the reader's interpretation.

Coulter's revision of "Oblomov" for radio is a fine example of his mastery of this style. The emphasis is entirely on voice. An announcer begins to tell the story of Oblomov while the sound effects, first established in the dialogue, can be heard: a distant tolling of a clock striking three, a door handle opening Oblomov's bedroom, a noisy flinging open of curtains as Zakhar tries to awaken his master. In the second act the sound effects for this romantic interlude in Oblomov's life are quite different: opera music, Olga singing, a military band in the park, birds singing, a doorbell ringing, the noise of fireworks, a dog barking—all signs of life. The third act introduces the dull sounds of passivity: heavy sighing, the slow rhythmical breathing of sleep, deepening at the end. Voices are very expressive; the dialogue simple and spontaneous. There are eight characters of whom only four have major roles; there are no long speeches nor long drawn-out scenes; frequent changes of scene with musical interludes add variety; the action is verbalized and the play complete in itself. This radio play was an international success; it was translated into many languages and broadcast in several countries on five continents. What contributed to its success? Perhaps the fact that Coulter understood and allowed "mind to speak to mind" even while the characters were saying something else. Radio was eminently suited to portraying the character of Oblomov and the audience was not at all puzzled. Indeed his gentle characterization made him beloved by his radio audience, particularly in Europe where the philosophical man is perhaps better understood than in a country such as America, where activity is of the essence.

The television version came sixteen years later and was produced by CBC "Playdate" on November 1, 1962. The television script proves that Coulter knew how to create in visual terms. He allows the images to replace dialogue and introduces more movement, insisting that the viewer see life before hearing it. In the final analysis, however, it was the director, David Gardner, who was responsible for the play's ultimate success. Herbert Whittaker who had seen the original stage play, remarked how much more difficult it is to present inertia before a camera. "Even a man asleep in bed is made to seem quite active by the time the camera has examined him."[14] He speaks of the radical changes made in the play to accommodate it to television—the form changing from farce to romance to pathos, without enough time for the audience to digest the author's intentions. However, he complimented David Gardner for endowing it with a Russian flavour, and the actors for their brilliant portrayals of character. Necessarily the critics' reviews emphasized the work of director and actors rather than the script of the author. In the final analysis it was judged a success.

IV Riel

Riel is another Coulter play that passed through the changes from stage to radio to television. The original stage play was given only a small amateur production by the New Play Society at the little theater in the Royal Ontario Museum in 1950; it was produced by Dora Mavor Moore with her son Mavor Moore in the title role. It was a good performance despite the small stage. However, Nathan Cohen said of Coulter's play: "For all the strength and subtlety of Mr. Coulter's play to become manifest, a production on the stage would be necessary. . . . It is an absolute disgrace that this brave and mythic drama . . . has gone unperformed."[15] Nathan Cohen is here referring to a major stage production, having heard and seen the radio and television performances. Sadly, Cohen did not live to see the triumphant major production at Ottawa's National Arts Centre in 1975, but we may be certain that his powerful support of the play in the past did much to influence producers.

The radio version of *Riel* was written by Coulter in 1951 and presented on the CBC "Wednesday Night" program. The French Canadian actor Franconi Levine played the role of Riel with power and passion. His eloquent, expressive voice added much to the radio production. Coulter rewrote the play for radio, limiting the cast, amplifying the voice aspect, simplifying the dialogue and plot, changing scene frequently, making the effort to appeal to the listeners' imaginations. The action had to be verbalized and sound effects established. A narrator-observer is introduced but the opening tends to be a bit boring as Coulter endeavors to set the historical background. Nevertheless, the radio version has the right combination of emotional content, sound effects, voice expression, imaginative elements, and credible "voices" like those of Joan of Arc, speaking to Riel, urging him to his destiny—a difficult thing to do on stage. Coulter, who was in London at the time, was not satisfied when later he heard the tape of the production because he felt that the voices were not subtle enough and the production insensitive. He referred to the need for silence on radio—the kind of pause that actually says a precise thing. He objected to the "voices" heard by Riel in his cell. Coulter said that "they were too loud, too close to the mike."[16] Despite this defect that was a director's mistake, the play itself was remarkably good on radio. Coulter had inserted mob singing, the sound effects of Orange lambeg drums in the distance, and an observer Lorne Greene who, throughout the play, movingly describes the changing scenes as one who is there actually seeing the events in Riel's life and thus adding a note of immediacy to the play. Between Part I and Part II—marked by the passage of fifteen years—Coulter asks for an intermission of fifteen minutes of music, entirely unrelated to the play. Again Coulter exhibits his sensitivity to a radio audience's needs. This 1951 radio drama was revived on CBC radio in 1968.

The television version was written in 1961 with the title role played by the brilliant actor, Bruno Gerussi. Here Coulter was preoccupied in emphasizing the visual content. The images take the place of dialogue; more movement is added; the close-ups of facial expressions add depth to the meaning. The television production opens with a dramatic film of Riel's gravestone, then moving back in time to the prisoner Riel in his cell, in a dream which is also a vision. Coulter thus establishes for the television audience the identity of Riel—the visionary martyred leader and founder of Manitoba. In his dream, Riel sees the past, fifteen years ago when government surveyors first indicated that the Métis would lose their land. The television camera immediately switches to André Nault's cabin in those days. The use of flashbacks is well done. There is a dramatic rising to the climax in the television version with emphasis on the fact that "the outlaw once more shapes the law." The television ending evokes a dramatic appeal with the recitation of the Lord's prayer; the gong sounding; André crying: "Alors . . . allez au ciel." Blackness becomes the black flag hoisted as the great bells toll and the Latin Requiem is sung by male voices. The young soldier in savage disgust expresses his interpretation of all this. There is then a cutback to Riel's grave, the stone covered with snow. It is a poignant, emotional ending, reminding one of the death and resurrection of Christ. John Ruddy, Drama critic for *The Telegram,* said it "was at once painless history, brilliant biography, action-packed adventure."[17]

Although the three versions of each of Coulter's plays are not all of equal caliber—some subjects being more readily adaptable to one form than another—the creative ability of Coulter in each of the three media is easily recognizable. There is, perhaps, no other playwright who produced three different versions of each of his plays. When one first tackles the Coulter archives, one is confused by the enormous output of the dramatist, and particularly by so many versions of the same play, frequently using different titles. However, when one sorts out the material and begins to read first the stage play, then the radio revision, and finally the television adaptation, one is impressed by the interesting progression of the work through its various phases and, like Coulter, one will settle finally for the initial stage play. But then neither radio nor television script is the finished art form. Only the tape and the film, in the final analysis, as only the live stage production, is the work of art.

CHAPTER 6

The Playwright as Poet and Librettist

T S. Eliot, in *The Sacred Wood* and in a surprisingly large
. number of articles, strongly advocated the necessity for returning to poetic drama. He advanced many arguments in its favor,
not the least being the legitimate craving of poets for the stage and
the desire of the public for verse plays. He emphasized how powerful was the intellectual stimulus of blank verse in Elizabethan
drama: when drama and poetry are combined, our imaginations are
the more deeply stirred. Eliot always believed that a poet would
turn necessarily to drama, and John Coulter was an admirer of
Eliot's work and words. Being first a dramatist, he reversed the
process and turned to poetry. The opportunity presented itself in
the form of commissions from CBC radio in Toronto in 1942 and in
1946 to write the librettos for two Canadian operas. Family
tragedies were at the root of his other efforts in this direction. A
book of poetry was initiated after the death of his close friend and
father-in-law, Dr. Alexander Primrose; a formal elegy was prompted
by the death of his colleague and friend, Dr. Healey Willan; a verse
drama, "Sleep, My Pretty One," was inspired by the suffering of
someone whom he dearly loved. These were all conscious efforts to
write poetic drama and poetry, rather than the unconscious poetic
rhythm that had infused his previous work.

I Transit Through Fire

During World War II, CBC radio in Toronto was producing
British ballad operas. John Adaskin, producer with the CBC staff,
suggested that writers be commissioned to compose a Canadian
opera. John Coulter and Healey Willan were approached as librettist and composer respectively. Healey Willan, Vice Principal of the

Toronto Conservatory of Music, was one of Canada's finest compos-
ers. Since ballad opera is too light for the crisis of war, which was the
theme chosen by Coulter, it therefore could not achieve what Coulter wanted. He offered to write what he described as a short opera
about young Canadians who, through war, integrated themselves
into the very community that had dispossessed them in the depression. In order to give Healey Willan the idea he wrote the prologue
and took it to the composer, who said: "Stand up and read it to me,
old man."[1] When Coulter had finished, Willan said, "Read it again!"
"Why?" asked Coulter. "Because," was the answer, "I compose on
plain chant and I want to hear your stresses." Then Willan impro-
vised harmony for it, and constructed the musical architecture for
the whole opera on hearing Coulter's plans. The melodic line was in
accordance with plain chant. Finally, he did the orchestration. Both
Healey Willan and Sir Ernest Macmillan, conductor, had sons who
had matured during the Depression. They said they had never understood what happened to their sons psychologically until they
read the libretto for *Transit Through Fire*.

Transit Through Fire is Coulter's social testament. In terms of a
Christian mythology, the young man in the opera divests himself of
his own personality and becomes the mystic. A priest, referring to
this opera, said to Coulter, "What you have managed is the Christian message—a denuding of the self as the self's consummation."[2]
John Middleton Murry's fondness for Keats' lines: "Those to whom
the miseries of the world / Are misery and will not let them rest,"
were constantly in Coulter's mind throughout the writing of *Transit
Through Fire*. The young man Howard Scott who sang the role of
Sergeant Thomson, sang it in his air force uniform. He was subsequently killed on his first air-training mission in World War II.

The concentration required to write this libretto was intense:
CBC gave Coulter less than three months to do it, and he spent
every waking moment with it. He listened to the language of the
students at the University of Toronto and imitated them. He inserted in it the most popular dance of that era, "The Lambeth
Walk." Coulter and Willan finally completed the opera to their
satisfaction in time for the date set by CBC radio, March 8, 1942. It
was a success, meriting enthusiastic reviews from music critics in
various parts of Canada. Christopher Wood, in an article in *The
Canadian Review of Music and Art*, said of it: "It is a fine libretto—a
noble idea well handled and most timely. The music fulfills the

implications of the libretto with a happy intimacy and the two unite in a work of genuine beauty and power."[3] Augustus Bridle of the *Toronto Star* called Coulter's work "A scathing scenario to music" and Healey Willan's composition, "the peculiar blazing technique of the composer as he vivifies the words of an opera that could be spoken as a play with wonderful effect. . . . In this both writers create a realism of despair."[4] Lucy Van Gogh, writing for *Saturday Night,* said of it: "A broadcasting job of extraordinary daring. . . . Dr. Willan's music is . . . often profoundly inspiring, and in John Coulter he seems to have found a librettist with just the right quality of poetic imagination and vivid eloquence to provide him with the verbal material he needs."[5] An article signed A. A. A. in the *Winnepeg Free Press* describes *Transit Through Fire* as

a great work brought forth by the war . . . a contribution to its genre of the first importance . . . of an impressiveness which . . . would compare to the accomplishment of Elgar or Vaughan Williams . . . an entity of . . . almost overwhelming beauty. . . . Words and music flowed as though from a single source of inspiration. The verbal and tonal interplay took one's breath away in the inevitability with which the shifting emphasis swung into focus or receded as artistic demands dictated. . . . The dominant impression was that the opera had that seldom attained inner form. . . . This is the grandest score which has ever been created in Canada.[6]

It is interesting to note the attention given by music critics to the libretto. Although all, without exception, praise Healey Willan's composition, an unusual comment keeps emerging—the libretto is, in itself, a drama that could stand alone! The difficulties of composing music for such a script are noted also. For example, an article in the *Toronto Star* observes: "Willan tackled a difficult text written by an expert in dramatic scenario."[7] Conducted by Ettore Mazzoleni, *Transit Through Fire* was revised for stage concert and presented at Convocation Hall, University of Toronto, in 1943. The libretto was published by Macmillan of Toronto in 1942. It was revised for CBC Television in Toronto in 1955.

It is a simple, straightforward tale, told with the utmost brevity, in a new method of expression, a series of episodic dialogues that combine the living newspaper technique which characterized Coulter's play "Mr. Churchill of England," produced a month earlier, with Brecht's epic theater technique later to be used in *Riel*. The characters are, like Brecht's, types or symbols: of youth in the Depression on the verge of war, of the university president mouthing platitudes, of the "beast" voicing the cynicism of the thirties, of the "Mystic" upholding self-sacrifice and detachment. The characters change with the exigencies of life, from superficiality to total dedication. Coulter is concerned here not with human nature but rather with human relations, in an effort to change the capitalistic picture of greed and indifference, to a socialism that would encourage genuine concern for one another. It is an opera based on history in the making, written in the middle of World War II and depicting the whole panorama of the Canadian scene in 1942. The audience is encouraged to remain detached in order to see more clearly the injustice portrayed and the social and moral implications of this opera. The effect is one of new wisdom: mankind is really the object of the investigation, and the characters, though defeated in the end, have become in a sense immortal. All this is Brechtian theater applied to opera. The living newspaper technique is evident in the rapid panoramic view, the series of vignettes, the colorful episodes, the excitement engendered, and the documentary and historical background.

For Brecht, the *story* is all important, unfolding like a tale in a number of individual scenes. *Transit Through Fire* is the story of William and Joan who take a retrospective view of their preparation for life since their graduation from university four years previously. In a remote Quebec skiing cabin Sergeant William Thomson is spending a brief leave with his wife, Joan, before returning to the horrors of war. A series of six scenes unfold in a dramatic exposition of a kind of "Look back in anger" savage satire. Scene 1 presents a number of college day reminiscences. Scene 2 is an ironic dialogue recalling the world that awaited them after graduation, its trivia and superficiality revealed in the dancing class. Scene 3 shows the struggle in the Depression to obtain a job, to retain one's college ideals before an increasing revelation of the greed and dishonesty that characterized the outside world. Scene 4 depicts William's "voices," like Joan of Arc's—the beast and the mystic—pulling him in opposite directions; the beast suggesting that he cast away any hope in democracy and settle for greed and selfishness as the only way out; the mystic encouraging him to denude himself of self in order to achieve salvation—the paradoxical Christian message of losing one's life in order to save it, of the dying seed that would yield much fruit. William tells Joan that he "had passed through transforming fire."[8] The evidence of this she saw in his face: "And when at last / You looked and smiled, / A new serenity— / Some spiritual grace— / As hushed and strange / As the grey of dawn / Shone in your face." Both Joan and William realize at last that love is the answer: "A future where love had begun. / And we found in love / future and past transcended. / all living things made one. / And we took wings and ascended / into the spring of the day. / Out of mortality / into the immutable moment / of eternity." Scene 5 is an ironic commentary recalling the ex-soldiers' treatment by the public when they return home from war. Scene 6 is a brief summation in which William suggests the answer when he proposes to Joan that they greet the end of leave "with a shrug and a wink"; presumably the shrug is typical of the world's irresolutions, and the wink, of life's tricks.

Transit Through Fire is an odyssey, a quest for life's meaning. Coulter described its poetry as: "Polemical, not poetry like *Deirdre*, a kind of verse like Eliot's 'patient etherised upon the table', a polemic piece in dramatic verse."[9] Coulter's poetic opera is a controversial dialogue echoing that long line of dialogues between self and soul of which "The Love Song of J. Alfred Prufrock" is a contemporary example. There is in *Transit Through Fire* the same desire to write verse drama, the same use of it to say something new to the reader, the same kicking against the goad, the same conservative and sometimes religious cast, but technically Eliot's style is of course far removed and above Coulter's. There is a subtly personal nature to the poetry of both men, and a willingness to accept, after all, the limitations of human nature. Both poets learned how to use speech idioms; both knew how to achieve striking effects from juxtaposing realism and fantasy. Sometimes the bitter ironical tone and the cynical self-criticism of the characters in Eliot's poetry would be echoed in Coulter's dramatic verse. Prufrock's eventual collapse back into mediocrity and William's "shrug and wink" have certain similarities of failure and acceptance. Both poets use a mask or persona. These personae comment on their environments, ironically and also compassionately. They mouth their authors' philosophies of life. In and beyond the poetry is a doctrine of moral order that cannot escape attention in both Eliot's and Coulter's dramatic verse. The same God that consciously inhabits Eliot's work

is unconsciously beneath the surface of Coulter's poetry. There is
the same mixing of religious and secular terminology and symbols.
Both raise questions of justice and injustice, of personal worth and
community responsibility. Certainly Coulter was indebted to Eliot,
but Coulter was not an imitator. His verse form, though minor, is
his own.

Transit Through Fire employs a short melodic line of free verse,
unrhymed, the caesura varying, with simile and metaphor used as
instruments of shock, as in Scene 3: "I looked upon what seemed / a
cynical obscene world, / and saw each counter and bench / and desk
as but a butcher's block / where the broken body of this society /
was hewn in pieces / amid the stench / of carrion / and the buzz /
of carrion flies." Over and over throughout the opera is the refrain
from the university president's convocation address which becomes
the theme and subject of irony: "Each man must find / his individual good / in seeking first the general good / of the community."
Coulter's words are blazing and powerful with a kind of prophetic
character to them. The whole is a symphonic poem rising to such
moments of grandeur as:

> There is a passage into life,
> out of limbo masquerading as life,
> that mystic way
> the spiritual adepts knew:
> to which I sought some clue
> through fasting and meditation.
> Yet found no guidance
> and was nigh despair
> when suddenly
> through the shuttered air
> a wind blew in my face,
> a radiance was about me:
> I stood in a desolate place
> by the foam of an occult tide
> where seabirds circled and cried
> of the cabbalistic secrets
> which only the dead can know,
> and in a lull of their crying
> it was as though I heard a voice
> the stricken voice
> of the Syrian mystic
> who died two thousand years ago.

Coulter's eloquence was illuminated by Willan's plain chant to such an extent that *Transit Through Fire* was called by critics Canada's first opera of professional caliber and the authentic voice of Canada, initiating a wave of interest in Canadian opera. As a testament of Coulter's whole social philosophy, it created a powerful impact on the people of Canada.

II   Deirdre

So successful was their first opera that the two collaborators, John Coulter and Healey Willan, were approached by CBC radio to write and compose another opera. This time Coulter chose a subject close to his heart—Deirdre. It is significant that his two operas have for their setting Canada and Ireland, even as his many plays may be so divided.

Deirdre, the story that has attracted more Irish poets and dramatists than perhaps any other, first suggested itself to Coulter when he was a young man, sharing a studio with Jimmy Sleator near the Abbey Theatre in Dublin. He had seen Deirdre interpreted by the three chief figures of the Irish Literary Revival: Yeats, A. E., and Synge. Yeats skillfully concentrated on the crisis of the Deirdre legend, introducing the musicians as a kind of Greek chorus who gave the highlights of the historical background, and also participated in the action. It was Yeats' second to last play, written for the National Theatre. A. E.'s (George Russell's) *Deirdre* was written for the Irish National Dramatic Company in 1902 and was its first offering. It is a beautiful little play, a delicate prose poem, but he failed to dramatize it convincingly. Synge's *Deirdre of the Sorrows*, not fully completed before his death, was presented posthumously in 1910 and proved to be more successful than either of its predecessors. Synge projected himself more than did Yeats or A. E. into his interpretation of the legend. He took the three parts of the tragic history of this section of the Red Branch Knights and humanized the legendary figures, approaching the story as a folk-dramatist, sensing the relationship between legendary Ireland and Gaelic Ireland. He used the speech of his peasant plays in a dignified and beautiful poetry. Naisi's fear of old age and death, echoing as it does Synge's same fear, lends a powerfully human quality to this universal tragedy of a fierce and primitive race.

It was natural that Coulter would want to follow his masters in writing a *Deirdre* of his own. His first attempt was made in a one-hour play for BBC radio entitled, "Conochar's Queen." Even before this, he had written a Deirdre play of five acts of blank verse which he later destroyed. It was not until 1946, when CBC radio approached Coulter and Willan for another opera, that he seriously tackled the Deirdre legend with the determination to write a successful poetic libretto. The result was far beyond his expectations. *Deirdre of the Sorrows*, his first title, finally changed simply to *Deirdre* out of respect for Synge's original title, was an immediate success. The libretto was published by Macmillan one year before the opera was produced. Healey Willan said of Coulter's libretto, "Coulter's text is one of the most beautiful things I have ever read."[10] Upon reading it, he said he immediately fell in love with Deirdre. Opera critics writing for newspapers and journals read the libretto and were most complimentary. *The Toronto Daily Star* of January 27, 1945, referred to the libretto in these words: "this barbaric and tragic old tale lives again with power, dignity and beauty." The *Vancouver Sun* of March 3, 1945, spoke of it as "The ancient tale . . . told in noble language and stately measure befitting the theme and period." The *Winnepeg Free Press* of February 24, 1945, remarked that "the author's meter fits perfectly to the tragedy of the legend." The *Halifax Chronicle and Mail Star* of February 10, 1945, gave Coulter a negative criticism when it described the opera as, "shorn to the bone of all but the bare narrative," whereas the *Hamilton Spectator* called it, "an excellent job in creating . . . libretto." The spring 1945 issue of *The Queens Quarterly* carried a review of it and pointed out that, "This retelling, despite a few metrical lapses, shows a sensitive response to the beauty of the fable. It is Mr. Coulter at his best." Finally, "The *Winnepeg Tribune* of June 9, 1945, made this somewhat wry comment: "It makes good reading which is almost revolutionary in a libretto for an opera."

The opera was produced on CBC radio's "Tuesday Night" program on April 20, 1946, and was greeted with high praise: its premiere performance was a success, as attested by the following sample comments. *Saturday Night*, March 24, 1945, (speaking of Coulter's earlier published libretto) observed that he "has brought to this work abundant fervor and no common stateliness. His sense of rhythm . . . is strong and of a sort to delight the composer." *Radio Vision*, April 27, 1946, noted that "*Deirdre of the Sorrows* . . . was received with deserved enthusiasm by music critics . . . a history-making event." *Newsweek*, April 29, 1946, stated that "*Deirdre of the Sorrows* is the first full length opera to be written and produced in Canada. . . . Appropriately enough, both Willan and Coulter set the opera in an aura of Celtic twilight strongly reminiscent of the half-lit world through which Maeterlinck's and Debussy's *Pelleas and Melisande* wandered to their undoing. 'It was a momentous production' summed up Thomas Archer, the distinguished critic of the *Montreal Gazette*." The *Globe and Mail*, April 30, 1946, mentioned that "the general reaction was good. Letters have poured into CBC. Ninety-eight per cent are complimentary." Finally, the earlier published libretto was reviewed for the *Montreal Gazette* on March 2, 1946, by Gordon LeClaire who said of it:

Mr. Coulter is able to conjure up with stark realism the authentic feeling and savor of the Irish scene. Furthermore his lines are permeated with the subtle rhythms and haunting overtones of the lilting Irish cadences, so that the whole opus is steeped in the fascinating atmosphere . . . created with an austere simplicity and a cumulative emotional power. . . . With terse dexterity of writing he brings his characters to pulsating life and the inevitable fate of the beautiful Deirdre . . . transpires with all the inexorable finality of Greek tragedy at its highest. The denouement . . . leaves one with a feeling of essential catharsis which only authentic tragedy is capable of evoking.

Deirdre of the Sorrows was published in book form by Macmillan of Canada in 1944 before the score by Willan had been completed. Coulter thought this an advantage for future radio audiences: if they could become familiar with the story first, when they heard the opera they might more fully understand it. There is no doubt that Coulter must have realized the quality of his poetry or he would not otherwise have permitted the libretto's early publication. It was fortunate he did so, because twenty years later the text was cut to two-thirds of its original length to adapt it for live stage. The first live theater performance of this opera was on April 2, 1965 at the Royal Conservatory of Music, Macmillan Theatre, the University of Toronto. The following year, on September 24, 1966, it was given its major production at O'Keefe Centre, Toronto, before an audience of over three thousand people.

Coulter had to cut his text drastically for live stage because those passages necessary for introduction, continuity, and identification on radio are superfluous on stage where the characters and setting can be seen. The *Globe and Mail* for September 22, 1966, had some interesting comments on this: "Much of the text, which differs from most opera librettos in its high literary quality, was originally devoted to explanations of actions that could not be seen by the radio listener. The production staff, with unheard of collaboration from composer Willan and librettist Coulter, trimmed it ruthlessly. . . . So much so, that the plot was occasionally obscured. Now our main problems are musical ones—trying to keep Willan's lush orchestration from obscuring the vocal line." As a result Coulter's libretto was, as Herbert Whittaker remarked in his review of the opera, "submerged . . . for more than three-quarters of the evening."[11] Whittaker felt that the opera lacked balance and it is reasonable to assume that the cause lay in the drastic cutting of the libretto, necessitated by the change from radio to live stage. Whittaker said in his article, entitled "Libretto Swamped by Willan Score":

. . . in this production . . . the weight of success falls where it generally does in opera, on the musical side. The welling evocations of the Willan score submerged the Coulter verse for more than three-quarters of the evening, a factor which often meant that the musical creation soared without sufficient support from the dramatic structure. . . . it is surely King Conochar who should centralize the action, for it is his seven-year obsession with Deirdre which gives the legend its touch of immortality. . . . His anguish, his authority and his passion were never on a scale to give the opera theatrical shape.

Kenneth Winters wrote in the *Telegram*, September 26, 1966, "John Coulter's book is impressive in its determination to be swift and simple, less impressive in its capitulation to implausibility." The final scene was particularly criticized, and the fault seemed to be the librettist's. William Littler of the *Toronto Daily Star*, September 26, 1966, remarked: "the writing is well sustained, save for the final scene." And John Kraglund of the *Globe and Mail* on the same date offered this comment: "If there was one scene that lacked musical clarity it was the final one, which should have achieved a sort of tragic grandeur but managed only to be confused. Perhaps the weakness lies with the score and the text . . . there is no reason for orchestra and singers (marvellous elsewhere) suddenly to lose control at this point." Obviously the weakness was caused by surgery!

The majority of the critics writing about the 1966 live stage production felt that Willan's music was dated and very much out of joint with contemporary operatic writing, reminding them powerfully of Wagner and Elgar. The latest criticism of *Deirdre*, written by Charles Acton for *The Irish Times*, Dublin, on September 14, 1973, as he reviewed it from a vocal score, found both words and music dated. Mr. Acton said:

A poor libretto can produce a great opera but a good libretto is nothing without the music. . . . Mr. Coulter's clearly written text is written too much in the spirit of the Irish Literary Revival. [But] For all that I have . . . said about the Celtic twilighteries, Mr. Coulter's libretto is, in fact . . . straightforward, honest, dignified, conversational writing which should come across admirably. . . . Mr. Willan's music is basically, interwar . . . some distance after Puccini. . . . There are many things against *Deirdre* but actual performance (by the Dublin Grand Opera Society) might just prove it to be a viable opera, in spite of a general impression of a chronicle rather than development of character during the course of it.

All this by way of saying that John Coulter's original libretto, as published by Macmillan in 1944, was far superior to the truncated version necessitated when converting it from radio to live stage. Since our interest here lies chiefly in Coulter's poetry, we shall consider only the opera as published in 1944.

The story of Deirdre, taken from the legends of the Red Branch Knights of Ulster, is a tragic tale of the foundling girl loved both by the old King Conochar of Ulster whose Druid priests forbid their marriage, and the young, handsome Prince Naisi. Deirdre is fated to bring death to herself and those who love her. She chooses to wed Naisi and they escape the King's wrath by taking refuge in Alba (Scotland). Conochar treacherously pretends to pardon them and so they return to Ulster after seven years, only to have Naisi slain. Deirdre takes her own life; Conochar's palace is set afire and Druid priests pronounce the judgment of the gods on him. The basic struggle is between Cathva, the Druid high priest, and King Conochar, who defies the gods' decree that he shall not marry Deirdre. Conochar's brooding revengeful spirit, his obsession with Deirdre's image, and his determination to fulfill his desires, provide the psychological motives for the story. Conochar's defeat is complete when the other clans rise against him. The opera ends as it began, with the Druid priestly rites. Lorne Betts, in reviewing the 1965 version of the opera said of it: "As a straight play one can imagine Coulter's work being successful but for an operatic libretto it seemed to be a hurried chronicle of events."[12] This is not true of the original edition of 1944 in which Coulter presents us with a finely molded and fully complete work of art, introduced by the Shannache, an old Irish storyteller, the bard of the old Gaelic school, who had to recite whatever legend the head of the table at the banquet chose. This role was taken by the radio announcer in the original text, but the entire role was removed from the live stage version. The ancient bard in the radio text skillfully and tactfully provides the visual background.

Lister Sinclair reviewed the original text for *Canadian Review of Music and the Arts* in 1945. In his opinion Coulter's *Deirdre of the Sorrows* is an extraordinarily good dramatic poem rather than a verse drama. He says of it:

The combination of tradition and musical necessity has rendered it virtually axiomatic that an opera libretto should be nonsense. . . . Fortunately Mr. Coulter's libretto . . . is, in fact, an excellent dramatic poem. It is proper to describe it this way rather than as a drama written in verse, because the work is not specially dramatic. . . . However it is most certainly poetic. The lyric interludes . . . are . . . passages of surpassing beauty. . . . Deirdre's lament . . . strikes me as one of the very best things of its kind that has been written. Moreover the poem has a most curious power of evoking a unique mood, quite in the manner of Debussy's *Pelleas et Melisande.*

Unlike Synge's *Deirdre of the Sorrows* which achieves its great beauty as a work of art through peasant idiom and folk tale genius, Coulter's version reached a dramatic peak through its poetry. Dignity, simplicity, and harmony of language contribute to produce an eloquent dramatic poem. In itself it is verbal music without the addition of an operatic score; yet the whole is achieved with great economy of words. Coulter himself said, "Economy of words. That is possibly the most essential characteristic of good librettowriting."[13] Like T. S. Eliot, he believed that the emotional stresses of contemporary life called for a heightening of language not possible in naturalistic dialogue. Coulter referred to this in an article he wrote at this time for *Theatre Arts:* "The spoken word of contemporary stage dialogue is no longer adequate to the needs of our day in the theatre. The deep ground-swell of feeling stirred by the emotional stresses of these turbulent years cannot be reflected on the stage in terms of naturalistic dialogue. . . . What is now needed is not simulated conversation but the depth and range, the utterance at large of dramatic poetry."[14]

Coulter has described how, as he proceeded to write *Deirdre,* "the loose prose rhythms of the dialogue tightened . . . into the regular pulse of verse and stanza"[15] as his own feeling for the Deirdre legend became more intense. A close textual study of the poem reveals the techniques he used to achieve his end. Figures of speech, appropriate consonant and vowel sounds, repetition, old bardic techniques, internal rhymes, parallelism, contrast—all combine to produce this love poem. The bard opens the play of Conochar and his ward with a fine use of onomatopoeia and alliteration: the very sounds of the words—druid, doomed, destruction— suggest an occasion of solemnity and death when one has defied the gods. Conochar's mockery of the druid priests at the beginning of the third act with the words, "Aha, Cathva"[16] is answered at the end by Cathva, the high-priest's curse, beginning with "Aha, Conochar" (72). Old bardic techniques include internal rhymes, internal repetition, long lines, questions and answers, and the splendor of voice at the beginning and end. Deirdre's Lament, in the third act, particularly adapts these old bardic techniques of prosody. Such internal rhymes as "Kilcuan," "rowan," and "ruin" (58), and internal repetitions as "come, is come," "tree, our tree," as well as Deirdre's question to Naisi beginning, like the *Canticle of Canticles,* with the words, "Ah, Naisi, my pride, my jewel, my only darling" (echoing the Canticle's "My love, my dove, my beautiful one"), serve to give liquid music to the verse while the changes in rhythm and caesura prevent monotony.

Coulter makes use of figures of speech without their becoming too apparent. Such examples as Conochar's reference to the priests as sheep or goats, "They bleat and prance" (4), suggest the damned, or the redeemed, depending on the viewpoint of the characters. Levercham, Deirdre's nurse, expresses Deirdre's inevitable fate and Conochar's flouting of the gods' decree, in a metaphor reminiscent of Coulter's early life: "He'd change the figured pattern on a web the gods are weaving. But the warp's laid in the loom, and the shuttle's moving" (18).

The imagery is vivid. The bard, in describing Ardan's dream, uses the simile: "with the sun on their shields and their spears / winding round through the glen / like a glittering river of fire" (19). Naisi refers to his dreams of Deirdre by using personification: "All night I lay and looked up at the stars; they were in league together, spinning night-fancies on a theme I know" (21). Deirdre speaks of Conochar's spies and fighters as "closing round us with their spears as thick as corn stalks in a harvest field" (27). When she refers to Conochar's chosen fighters, he replies: "Death is their trade and they are skillful tradesmen" (34).

The climax of the opera when Naisi decides to return home is more credible than Synge's play. Coulter gives Naisi a motive familiar to himself—the loneliness of the exile who at last is offered an opportunity to return to Ulster, his native land. Synge offers his personal interpretation of Naisi's motives for returning, as a fear of remaining for a lifetime in a place where both will grow old and weary and where he might lose his delight in Deirdre. Deirdre overhears him and therefore, considering death preferable to a loss of love, encourages him to accept Conochar's invitation. Synge's own fear of his imminent death probably suggested this motive.

Coulter often uses contrast in his libretto. For example, in Act III, scene 1, Conochar is given a long aria, with stern lines and prophetic voice, proclaiming the dire events to come. The tone is one of anger and revenge. Immediately following this in scene 2, Naisi, Ardan, and the Clansmen sing a short-lined happy song anticipating the warm welcome they expect from their kinsmen in Ulster. There is contrast between scenes 1 and 2 in Act I. Scene 1 prophesies the doom of Conochar and the fate of Naisi in the ceremonial rites of the druid priests around the sacred tree, beside the sacred well—suggesting the migration of the lost tribes of Israel in the desert country. The lines are long, the tone menacing. Scene 2 is a happy, light contrast—Deirdre telling her nurse that she has seen Naisi and fallen in love with him. Although this passage is written in short prose lines, the rhythm suggests poetry as much of Coulter's prose not infrequently does. An example of this is Deirdre's explanation to her nurse of her day: "I've been a long time in the woods this day, but I was happy, Levercham, oh, happy as a rider on a high cloud, coasting above the mountain in the blue sky and sun" (14).

There are four lyric interludes in this opera, two each in Acts I and III. The quality of the poetry in these interludes is so superior to most operatic arias that each can justly be said to be a lyric poem in its own right. The initial interlude belongs to Deirdre who sings of her first meeting with Naisi. The imagery makes use of color:

"yellow yorlin," "blue gap," and "black was his hair" (14). The second interlude is Naisi's, who surveys the scene at dawn and sings of his love for Deirdre, ending with the lines:

> Bright day and dark night are as one; I live in the drift of a dream
> Where my love is the light of the sun and the quiet of the stars
>   and the moon,
> And a music that lifts me and soars and sets my lips laughing
>   and lilting
> And sets my feet dancing and running, as I run now to Deirdre,
>   my love. (20)

King Conochar sings the third interlude in which repetition is used to emphasize the mood of revenge. The last interlude is the much publicized Deirdre's lament as she reflects on their idyllic life together and contemplates leaving Alba for a lonely grave.

Coulter has projected a mood of Celtic melancholy, in an exquisite love fated to die, which persists throughout this dramatic poem and is responsible for its unity and beauty. The voice is the voice of the exiled Ulsterman, with all its haunting qualities of loneliness, anguished love, and mournful acceptance of the inevitable. The lack of humor and the unmistakable dour note mark this lyric drama as uniquely Ulster. Whether one calls it a long dramatic poem, a verse play, or a radio opera, *Deirdre of the Sorrows*[17] has met the requirements for a work of literary art.

III *"Sleep, My Pretty One"*

W. B. Yeats had said in his book, *Plays and Controversies*, that "In time, I think, we can make the poetical play a living dramatic form again. . . ."[18] T. S. Eliot had remarked, "Surely there is some legitimate craving, not restricted to a few persons, which only the verse play can satisfy."[19] When the verse play began to appear again, Christopher Fry had noted: "I lay the acceptance of poetry in the theatre nowadays to two things. One is the reaction to the long hold of 'surface realism'. The other is that the world seems rather cut down a bit. . . . And poetry provides something people lack and wish for: a richness and a reaffirmation."[20] Not only was John Coulter a disciple of Yeats, Eliot, and Fry, but he had himself always believed that the verse play would free him from what he called "the crippling limitations of the effort to simulate actual naturalistic speech. . . . This hope of release lay in the success . . . of T. S. Eliot and Christopher Fry with their verse plays."[21] Coulter felt that neither had wholly succeeded; Eliot had pitched his verse too close to prose and Fry had forgotten the play in the intensity of his verbal acrobatics. Coulter said in his memoirs: "Between these two I had the temerity to attempt a dramatic verse which should be effectively, and affectingly, theatrical." He therefore wrote the verse play, "Sleep, My Pretty One." Based on a real situation involving someone he dearly loved, Coulter felt assured that the theme was realistic, although the type of play he planned to write would not be realism. His aim was to attempt a verse play somewhere between the vestry-clinic verse of T. S. Eliot and the sensuous verse of Christopher Fry.

The play as it finally emerged has proved itself to be the most controversial of Coulter's works. Critics either disliked it intensely or became obsessed by it. Sir Laurence Olivier said that he had to drive himself through the first act but in the second act he had been caught and held and had gone on to the end. He said: "There is something very strange in it, formidable and frightening, which I could not get hold of or define. It has a certain dark power. It reminds me in some way of *Hedda Gabler*."[22] He therefore bought an option on it but never produced it. Murry MacDonald, a respected London director, said he thought the soliloquies in it "unmatched except in Shakespeare."[23] Yet a critic for the *Canadian Commentator* said of the actress who played Flora, "She had to fight her way through long soliloquies on stage which would have made an accomplished Shakespearean quail."[24] The same critic spoke of the plot as "well-worn," the denouement as "wildly melodramatic," and the dialogue as "the main fault of the play." Sybil Thorndike called the play, "Absorbingly interesting," while a critic for the *Toronto Daily Star* said that "the would-be poetic language . . . doesn't work."[25] Tyrone Guthrie remarked in a letter to Coulter: "I certainly think that "Sleep, My Pretty One" has a good deal of neurotic force and humor. . . . I felt it was like a Compton Burnett novel."[26] Both Edith Evans and Bette Davis complimented Coulter on his writing but neither liked the play. Bette Davis said, "I have an impression that one would not care too much about any of the characters or their problems."[27] Yet Coulter has always considered "Sleep" one of his best plays. In a letter to Sir Laurence Olivier, dated May 18, 1951, Coulter said: " 'Sleep' was written in a conscious effort to find a place between Fry and Eliot—between the matchless lyricism of Fry's imagination and writing, and the urbane clinic-confessional of Eliot—a place for dramatic verse which should be charged with dramatic tensions to the fullest degree of which I am capable—what might perhaps be called *theatrical* dramatic verse."

The controversy aroused by "Sleep" has never resolved itself. Coulter rewrote the play several times, tightening up the dialogue, revising the ending, sacrificing some of the soliloquies and the final scene between Flora and Quinn for the sake of a more direct telling of the story. Yet the play has never been offered a major production. It was given a rehearsed reading at the Royal Court Theatre and St. James Theatre in London in 1954 with Irene Worth as Flora; and it had its premiere performance at Centre Stage in Toronto, April 14–22, 1961. It was revised for CBC radio. A retelling of my own gradual awakening to the play's artistic form is revealing, to say the least. At first the play seemed to lack that inner fire with its outward expression of vitality of poetic language that marked Coulter's more successful plays. It would seem that in his efforts to achieve a certain art form which had gripped his imagination, he had let go of the soul of the play. Indifference and a certain coldness, a frigidity of form, had, it appeared to me, stifled the genuine emotional drive that had originally inspired it. However, giving it a slower, more concentrated reading, I was at least able to distinguish the efforts made by Coulter to place an art form between Eliot and Fry.

The play revolves around the characters of Anne and her stepmother, Flora. The impossibility of Anne's accepting her father's choice of a new wife after the death of her beloved mother, heightens the strained relationship between the two women and causes the neurotic buildup, to the catastrophe of Anne's suicide. The slow rhythmic evolution of poetic language shorn of almost all metaphoric adornment is in itself an inexorable forewarner of doom. The play seems to take place on two planes at once, suggesting a sense of action on two different levels, the area of Anne's individual dilemma, and the larger universal tragedy of hopelessness in the face of death. It is reminiscent of something Coulter said to Nathan Cohen on the CBC "Tuesday Night" program, December 3, 1968, as he was being interviewed on "Oblomov." Cohen asked him which of his plays he liked the best and Coulter had answered "Oblomov" because, he said "he stands for something that is very close to my own way of feeling about things . . . not the man of inaction but the civilized man who has seen everything, done everything, and is aware of the absurdity of existence in the world and is simply going to back away from the contest." It is to Cohen's credit that he challenged this affirmation of despair by the words, "Is existence absurd?" And Coulter replied; "It's absurd in the sense that when some life suddenly comes to an end, you know what's behind the whole idea of existentialism and the play of the absurd. Human existence is absurd." Cohen's triumphant reply was, "Human existence is ennobling!" In considering "Sleep, My Pretty One" it is well to remember Coulter's affinity for existentialism and the theater-of-the-absurd.

The language is not realistic imitation; yet it is a full expression of feeling and sensibility. There is, despite Coulter's despair, no apparent personal philosophizing in the drama. The human soul, when in the grip of intense emotion, strives to express itself in verse in a kind of ritual which conveys the dominant tone of hatred and despair. It is symbolic of contemporary life as Coulter sees it. The action is stylized as the voice of the poet attempts to create a kind of third voice rising to moments of lyrical intensity. The universal spiritual significance of the drama creates a kind of myth in which Anne's guilt is shared and made general: there seems to be another connection with cosmic forces above and beyond us at work in our lives. Coulter's verse achieves a stark simplicity in keeping with this mood. The clairvoyance of the maid, Sheila, is suddenly ours, as we too seem to approach a vision beyond time, in a drama that has suddenly become highly sophisticated, and which has introduced a metaphysical dimension unexpected at the outset. Coulter has sacrificed all poetical devices to achieve this end. The verse is flexible enough to admit an ordinary conversational tone, yet the flowing rhythm is maintained to prevent the reader from sinking into realism. The impassioned insight of Anne with her sudden shifts of thought and feeling bears witness to a deeper reality and her mad obsession causes the final catastrophe and denouement. Throughout the verse drama Coulter's poetry is lucid, capable of the greatest precision and distinction. Much of this technique he has learned from a close study of Eliot's verse drama. In the work of Christopher Fry he found abundant examples of the creation of effects toward which he was working, an alive and contemporary idiom, an intricate rhythm and irregular blank verse as well as a repetition of words and phrases to convey a sense of inner tension. Undoubtedly Coulter has, in "Sleep, My Pretty One," reached that nice balance between Eliot and Fry toward which he was striving.

"Sleep, My Pretty One" is a difficult work for a critic to assess who has not seen the play, but must depend on a reading of it. What happens is that the critic gives it a first reading in a straightforward manner, thinking the play to be realistic. The result is contempt for anything so obviously melodramatic. Then it occurs to the reader that he just might be dealing with a play in the vein of romanticism and symbolism. A second reading sheds more light on its worth. Still not satisfied, a third reading finally reveals it in its true light—a kind of surrealistic dream dialogue, with theater-of-the-absurd mannequin characters combined in a realistic setting. Coulter has evidently stumbled on a new combination of older techniques because the exigencies of his play demanded this type of handling. The dialogue is a dream dialogue expressing subconscious mental activities without the usual fantastic or incongruous imagery that generally accompanies surrealism. Furthermore, it is spoken in a normal realistic setting. We therefore conclude that it is realism. Only in a production of the play with the dialogue spoken as it should be, in tones symbolizing the subconscious mind, will an audience, educated to surrealism, understand and appreciate it.

An interesting statement made by Coulter himself will shed light on this. Coulter is referring in his memoirs to his immense satisfaction with Irene Worth's rendition of Flora's part at the March 28, 1954, reading of "Sleep" at the Royal Court Theatre in London: "Irene Worth was superb—but superb less as a substantial character than as a voice while, toward the close, with a sort of desperate, defeated gaiety, she drifted about on the darkening stage gathering from the air and making audible the melancholy, the empty desolation, the doom—the ambient poetry of the piece, enveloping and inescapable as fear in a haunted room. There was little applause. There was incomprehension."

Both Flora and Anne are simply voices out of a dream world, mannequins in a theater-of-the-absurd. There are in this play definite influences of August Strindberg's departure from realism and naturalism in his *A Dream Play* which places it in the whole existential movement of the theater-of-the-absurd. Strindberg consciously attempted to use the structure and logic of a dream without any attempt to approximate reality, at the same time destroying time as a continuum. Each character seems to be isolated. The themes of hatred, cruelty, and love form the cluster around which *A Dream Play* revolves. A senseless punishment is substituted for love. Coulter's play, *Sleep*, has similarly the qualities of a dream, of characters drifting in and out, saying illogical things, in an atmosphere where time is destroyed. The characters seem isolated; their conversation has the quality of soliloquy because they are unable to reach or answer each other. The same Strindbergian cluster of hatred, cruelty, and love form the theme of "Sleep." Shadowy in outline and fluid in form, both *A Dream Play* and "Sleep" emerge out of a world of delusion and nightmare. Strindberg's revolt is existential, directed against the meaninglessness of life and its contradictions; Coulter's rebellious attitude toward life has had similar roots, but it has been directed in a less paranoiac, more reasonably disciplined fashion. Yet both men resolve their problems in a kind of melancholy and fatalism. As Strindberg's most characteristic tone can be heard in his later plays, notably *A Dream Play*, so Coulter's distinguishing trait is to be found in "Sleep." In Strindberg's drama can be located the origin of psychology in the modern play. Coulter inherited this and projected it in Anne's neurotic madness, the subtle references to incest, and her inability to adjust to her father-lover's taking a second wife. Strindberg seems to be saying of *A Dream Play* that in death only are contradictions resolved. Coulter has his character, Anne, resolve her sufferings in suicide and her father's in death.

It is not difficult for audiences to place Strindberg's play in the nonrealistic realms of the dream world. They were aided by the fantasy and imagination of stage scenery which was expressionistic in character—vivid, lush, paradisiacal, or filled with the horror of nightmare. Coulter, on the contrary, allows his "Sleep" to take place in the most commonplace, realistic settings of a middle-class home. The only hints we have of surrealism are elements of dream in the characters' dialogue and isolation. Reality in the scenery and in the characters of father and doctor seem to be outside the dream pattern altogether. Just as surrealistic painting used meticulously realistic techniques in a kind of concrete irrationality while exploring the subconscious mind and delineating the more real world beyond the real, so Coulter used the outward theatrical trappings of realism to explore the inner reality of the subconscious mind of Anne. Although surrealism produced no drama of merit, it did result in a new dramatic form—the theater-of-the-absurd.

Two important elements of theater-of-the-absurd emerge in Coulter's play. The first is that combination of dialogue and character which immediately provides the play's strongest point—the creation of atmosphere. Recall Olivier saying of "Sleep": "There is something very strange in it, formidable and frightening which I could not get hold of or define . . . a certain dark power." Pinter's plays have that characteristic of immediately creating atmosphere and creating it imperceptibly for the audience. For example, in *Old Times*, one is gradually made aware of the nostalgia as well as the agony of recalling old times in the very opening scene when the shadowy presence of the old girl friend is there on stage, unobserved—there, yet not there. She never opens a door or steps into the room but we are subconsciously aware of her presence and all she symbolizes. The opening scene of "Sleep" likewise presents us with atmosphere—the hatred and dread of the rival, Flora, caused by Anne's incestuous love of her father. The poetic dialogue mesmerizes us into a dream world which is more real than the real world. Flora is not on stage but her presence is there.

The second element of theater-of-the-absurd is the unreality of the characters. They are mannequins, mere voices; and we never become absorbed in them as real people. Instead, we become obsessed by the subconscious mind which is saying something so essential and universal that we are vitally moved by it. The characters in "Sleep" are mannequins. Coulter tells us in his memoirs: "Irene Worth was baffled in her effort to find 'some reality' for the character." Obviously neither dramatist, director, nor actress was aware of the theater-of-the-absurd elements in this play. Written before 1951, "Sleep" had its first reading at the Royal Court Theatre in London in 1954. This was one year before Beckett's play, *Waiting for Godot*, made its first appearance in London. The genius of Beckett must have appealed to Coulter, particularly the anguish of existentialism in Beckett's work and the Oblomov-like characteristics in his behavior; his apathy, for example, that kept him in bed till mid-afternoon. Beckett wrote in French in order to discipline his style, a difficult thing for an Irishman. Coulter, in *Sleep*, pared down his style to the core. Beckett's first and greatest theater-of-the-absurd plays were not written until the period between 1945–1950. Iones-

co's first theater-of-the-absurd play, *The Bald Soprano*, was produced in French in 1950. His great play, *The Chairs*, acted with a
naturalness of detail, was entirely incomprehensible to most of the
audience when it was first presented in 1952 in Paris. Genet's first
play to be produced was *The Maids* in 1947 in Paris. All this is to say
that the conventions of this new style had not yet reached the
English-speaking theater much before Coulter's play, "Sleep, My
Pretty One," had its first reading in London. It is therefore understandable that directors and actors alike did not comprehend it. For
Coulter it is just another example of his propensity for anticipating a
new dramatic convention, as he had done four years earlier with
Brecht's epic theater in *Riel*.

"Sleep, My Pretty One" is, therefore, the result of a cross-
breeding of the dream convention, surrealism, theater-of-the-absurd, and verse drama with a strain of realism in the setting: Its
timing was bad, appearing as it did before these new conventions in
theater had become familiar. It is unfortunate that it has never been
recognized nor given a production. Coulter says of it in his memoirs:
" 'Sleep's' chances of being produced are over . . . unless there
should one day be a renewed interest in restoring to playwright and
audience the pleasure of rhetoric employing the full range of non-
conversational vocabulary in non-realistic plays."

IV The Blossoming Thorn

In his youth, Coulter had attempted to write poetry, but he was
unsure of his talent in this medium and soon abandoned it. What he
seemed unaware of was his poetic rhythm even in his most commonplace prose pieces. The dialogue in his plays, were it arranged
in the poetic line, would indeed be free verse, as was demonstrated
in Chapter 3 where a comparison was made between Brecht's *Good
Woman* and Coulter's *Riel*. Obviously Coulter was not cognizant of
the fact that he was writing verse. He tells us that his first serious
attempt at poetry was for the two operas for which CBC commissioned him to write the librettos. The enjoyment he derived from
writing these encouraged him to tackle a book of poetry, *The Blossoming Thorn*. The death of his father-in-law, other subsequent
family deaths, his wife's sudden illness with polio—all in the same
year, 1944, cast him into such grief that his only salvation seemed to
be in writing poetry. The book was published by the Ryerson Press
in 1946 and was not received with any great acclaim. The poetry is

derivative of Yeats and other contemporaries of Coulter's, but it does have a charm of its own, a kind of haunting quality as it sings of the sorrows of the exiled man, the bereavement of those who have lost loved ones, the seasonal changes that accompany and revitalize our moods.

Coulter was the only Canadian poet writing under the direct influence of the Irish literary renaissance. His style and mood can be traced back to it although the themes are Canadian. He interprets for Canadians the natural beauties of their land in such poems as "Swift Canadian Spring," "Muskoka," and "Robin Singing." He writes of the "sheep bell tinkle of streams" and "the goose-flight wedge splitting the northern winds" in what he calls a renewed romanticism. Some of his poems seem experimental but, although a complete mastery of form may sometimes be lacking, there is a fine delicacy of workmanship and a subtlety of rhythm in many of them. Coulter approached the writing of poetry the way a newly ordained priest approaches the altar to say Mass for the first time—with great reverence, trepidation, self-depreciation, and an awful awareness that he is suddenly waist-deep in the eddying stream of a ritual with roots deep in a culture that is some two thousand years old. Coulter never said his Mass with the freedom of the self-confident man but leaned instead on the rituals of the past. In his "Apprentice's Note for Fellow-Craftsmen"[28] he expresses this idea: "In this belief one sets out, submitting oneself to the guidance of the masters, respectfully attempting work in the old patterns so that the hand may be trained and imaginative energy put to the test. The apprentice makes this bid for his 'footing' among the journeymen. . . . Even the apprentice may be uneasily aware that he is ill-served by some verse-form which he is trying to use, some pattern wrought for their own needs by masters whom he has admired. . . . But he may find that the current fashion serves him no better."

Coulter called for a new romanticism but he was not about to create a new form himself. He therefore clung to the old and his poetry has merit despite its borrowed forms. There is, for example, the imagist poem in the style of Ezra Pound—"Old Man in Bed"; a few traditional elegies, "Elegy I (For Alexander Primrose)" which uses the deceptive plainness of Robert Frost in similes like this one: "As a well worn garment is camphored and folded away / To what resurrection? we coffined and laid in clay" (1). He compares Dr. Primrose to an aging tree, echoing the nineteenth-century romanti-

cists. "Elegy II" (for Elizabeth Primrose, his mother-in-law) is also a
reflection of the romantics as he speaks directly to her in such
metaphors as "your broken Lute" and "the lamp is shattered" (4).
These elegies are too derivative and too full of clichés to merit
praise. In his "Farewell in Fall" he echoes Edna St. Vincent Millay
in such phrases as: "I cannot hold / This glory" (6). His choice of
words is unfortunately a rephrasing of many good poets before him,
yet, strangely enough, though the words seem ordinary, the
thought evoked is occasionally quite extraordinary, like the reading
of some commonplace prayer that suddenly lifts the soul to a new
contemplation of old truths. So the words in "Farewell in Fall" take
on a heightened meaning in the first six lines, only to fall into the
depths in the last four lines. It reminds one of the undulating rise
and fall of the ocean tides. The dourness of the Ulsterman can be
perceived in such poems as the short "Rueful Song" (7) bemoaning
lost youth; "Rendezvous Revisited," (8) lamenting the failure of a
loved one to return; "Dirge" (9) " (9) expressing the grief of mourn-
ers; "Spring in Autumn" (10), mocking hope; and "The Bereaved,"
emphasizing the finality of death in the faintly Dickinsonian words
of "Closed the shutters, barred the door" (11).

Coulter's nature poems invariably end on a desolate note of part-
ing and death. Many of these are reminiscent of his idyllic island,
Dahwamah, in Muskoka, Ontario, where he and his family still
spend long serene summer months. There in the quiet of a twenty-
seven acre lushly beautiful island, Coulter could find the solitude
and quiet needed for his work. In the poem, "Autumn Song and
Epitaph" he speaks of Dahwamah (Indian for sister) in these lines:
"Suddenly from a grey sky the sun shone on our island/as a hand
sweeping the bright strings of a harp, and we laughed in the
summer/noon, our spirits also kindling in warmth and light" (14).
He mourns the death of autumn in "First Snow" (15) as he offers a
metaphor of its burial: "exuberant gay leaves / shed, / out of aspiring day / down fled, / down the descending gyre / to the last folding
wings / in the night of the dead." But spring awakens everything
again as in his poem "The Swift Canadian Spring" (19), he writes:
"Lo, shot from the gleaming bow / of spring / an arrow of wild geese
cleaves / northward. / And suddenly the lawns are green / and
snowdrop and crocus have been / and are gone / and the bare
boughs are heavy with leaves." His poem entitled "Muskoka" (20) is
particularly evocative of that northern Ontario lake country. He

speaks of the "unsealing" of the wharves in April from the iced shores, the "bleaching stones," the "blue sunglitter" of the lake, summer's "sunheavy days," September's "wreathed moon" and winter's winds "in widening sickle-swathes the swift dark wings of the squall."

Perhaps his best poems are his three "Immigrant-Exile" poems I, II, and III. These three sonnets, in an irregular metric line of intricate rhythm, bespeak the paradox of the exile-immigrant who, seeking a home in the new land, finds "his roots still burrowing for their native clay" (27). In I and III he is compared to a tree uprooted and replanted. In II he is the wanderer on "the face of the waters." The final couplet in each sonnet offers little or no hope to the exile. In I he is a dying tree, "the dark boughs of his mind / Stand withered in mid-summer, spectral in an alien wind" (27). Sonnet II describes him at the window of the ark waiting for that "token wing" or "the grounding of the Keel" (28). Sonnet III refers to the rootless tree shedding its withering leaves, and the exile hearing in his heart "the contradictory call / Of curlews on the hills of Donegal" (29).

On the whole, Coulter's poems in *The Blossoming Thorn* are serious in tone, straightforward in theme, and colorful in imagery. There is a simplicity about them that bears a certain charm, despite the fact that they are, on the whole, echoes of an earlier age in poetry, reflections of Yeats' romanticism and the Irish renaissance.

Not included in *The Blossoming Thorn* was an elegy written some twenty years later, "Lament for Healey Willan." This was inspired by the death of his friend and collaborator in opera, who died in 1968. It is a traditional elegy in a serious, almost proselike, line with faint overtones of T. S. Eliot in Coulter's description of Willan's fastidiousness: "He burnished his fingernails, wore spats." His tender affection for Willan is obvious in such lines as, "I lay my hand on his hand / and turn from his bedside / lamenting the cessation of Healey Willan, / desolate beyond even the desolation / I had anticipated." It is an elegy in which the poet lays bare his own lack of faith in immortality as he says, "Ah Requiem!/ What requiem for that which is not." Coulter recreates the human qualities of Willan in such a warm and evocative description as, "his nature was gentle, warm, responsive; / an intuitive creature of quick perception / and touching childlike suspicions / and trust and a chuckling mischievous / sense of humor. His mind was a rich / compendium of hilarious bawdy tales." The elegy is a fine tribute to a great musician and friend. It was printed in the *Monthly Letter* of the Arts and Letters Club for February 19, 1968, and quoted in the periodical *Opera Canada* in its spring issue of that year.

With the death of Healey Willan Coulter ended his work as a librettist. With the final polishing up and still unproduced verse drama, "Sleep, My Pretty One," Coulter lost heart in the poetic drama even as he had ceased to write poetry after the publication of *The Blossoming Thorn.* He was too good a literary critic not to see the weaknesses in his formal poetry. He had said in that *Apprentice's Note for Fellow Craftsmen:* "The apprentice makes his bid for his 'footing' among the journeymen, fearful that the answer may be 'No'; and if 'No' should indeed be the answer, and if self-criticism should concur, he may decide that his first book of verse shall also be his last" (53). That first book was also his last book of poetry.

He therefore settled for prose once again as he prepared to write his memoirs, "In My Day." The memoirs record the story of his personal and literary life—a life rich in its associations with some of the most colorful literary and theatrical persons of the twentieth century. Paradoxically, what he once again unconsciously did was to write the memoirs in some of the richest poetic prose of his long life. His background as a prose writer goes further back into his literary career than even his work for theater. Coulter as a young man wrote articles and sketches for the Ulster newspapers, feature programs for the BBC radio in Belfast and London, and sent literary criticism to learned journals. Among his prose writings can be counted a novel, a biography, numerous essays and a few excellent short stories, a large body of literary criticism, and finally his memoirs. The reading of these numerous prose pieces offers one a rich glimpse into his background.

CHAPTER 7

Coulter's Nondramatic Works

BEFORE John Coulter had ever used a pen to sketch his verbal pictures, he had first been taught the craft of art—canvas, brushes, and painter's tools. His masters had trained him at the Belfast School of Art to observe, with the sharpness of vision of painters, the people and things around him; only then was he permitted to transfer to canvas what he had truly seen. Coulter's six years at the School of Art were his best preparation for writing: his colorful short stories and travelogues, his essays, memoirs, novel, and biography all bear witness to the power of insight derived first from the power of eyesight. What he saw, he transferred to his readers so that they too could see. In his weekly CBC radio program "Books and Shows" he said on March 9, 1943: "To see people and things in a special way is based on visual alertness, on the unusual power of seeing, truly *seeing*, what you're looking at; a trained sensitiveness to the visual aspect of the world-around—with a consequent habit of mind in which thought, the first stimulus to a train of thought, is most often in the impact of something seen."

I Essays

Although Coulter chose a wide variety of subjects for his numerous essays and articles, these for the most part remained within the area of literature, theater, and the arts. Perhaps his greatest contributions were his provocative articles on Canadian drama and Canadian theater. He tells us in his memoirs that he was influenced, not only by the writers of the Irish literary renaissance but by such British authors as Ruskin, Pater, and D. H. Lawrence. He mentions especially his indebtedness to John Middleton Murry whose literary criticism "stirred and delighted me as illuminatingly reasoned expositions of felt insights, frequently of penetrating depth and subtlety."[1] Coulter's literary criticism is sharp, perceptive, and to the point; his film and play criticism is professional in its insight; his art criticism communicates the mood or excitement of the critic giving his immediate reactions on first viewing the paintings.

The first bit of writing Coulter had published and was paid for, when he was quite young, was not in the area of the arts but in sports. Printed in *Saturday Night*, it was entitled "Rugger versus Soccer," Coulter's address when he wrote this was Crieve, Strandtown, Co., Down. The theme was that soccer employs head and feet only, making it a sport for spectators as well as players, while rugger is instinctive and physical, a sport chiefly for players. As an initial piece of writing it is of good quality, and, in fact, makes some interesting points. As a young man he also reviewed sports events, particularly tennis matches, for *The Belfast Telegraph* and *Saturday Night*. Of Wallace Myers' tennis reviews in *The Daily Telegram*, Coulter says in his memoirs, "They had for me some of the pleasure to be had from perceptive book reviews and I set out to emulate them." Young Coulter's accounts, both in newspapers and on radio, were stimulating and original. In describing the tennis tournaments he combined insight into technique with a psychological perception of the players' feelings and motivations. Many years later, when he was giving his weekly radio program "Books and Shows" on CBC radio in Toronto, the experience he had gleaned was used to advantage. These broadcasts, which extended from June 16, 1942, to March 30, 1943, were challenging talks on books, plays, movies, and art shows. Among the writers, for example, whose works he criticized was Aldous Huxley, about whom he says, "He has come at last to value the 'non-attachment' of the mystics as the way of wisdom." He goes on to remark that both Huxley and John Middleton Murry reached identical conclusions, "that there is but one way of progress for mankind . . . to break through the illusory world of appearances into the reality of . . . the immediate knowledge of God . . . the identification of self with the immanent and transcendant."[2] He is insightful when he reviews, for example, Emily Carr's autobiography, *The Book of Small.* Coulter says of her style that she has, "that rare thing, the indubitable word of the quickened and quickening imagination, luminously and beautifully at play upon the world" (December 15, 1942). Reviewing in Toronto an art show, "Americans 1942," from the Museum of Modern Art in New York, he says that what was specifically American about these paintings was the independence, individuality, eagerness, sense of stress, and, added to this, "an underlying spiritual perturbation or tension . . . and this I must call religious . . . the elemental emotion of religion" (December 22, 1942).

On January 19, 1943, he broadcast over his program "Books and Shows" a controversial talk on the arts in Canada. His theme was that there was a Canada but no Canadians in the sense that there were Irish in Ireland or English in England. He used what he called "shindies," a half-serious but deliberately provocative argument. He had already written several essays on the lack of Canadian drama. His talk provoked numerous responses in letters and phone calls. The following week he replied to his accusers: "As for browbeating, if I hit any brows it was a complete mistake. . . . There is after all a great difference between hitting a brow and hitting a vacuum."

Among his more provocative articles encouraging Canadians to write Canadian drama was one that appeared in *Theatre Arts Monthly* for July, 1938, entitled "The Canadian Theatre and the Irish Exemplar." He argued that he was a visiting Irishman whose notion of values in theater had been acquired at the Abbey Theatre, Dublin, where nearly all the plays were deeply rooted in Irish life; and he had assumed that this would also be true of Canada. The theater he had found in the Canada of 1938, however, was scarcely Canadian in content; it was the Dominion Drama Festival, drawing together the diverse communities of Canada through the production of British and European plays. The Festival should, he felt, encourage the writing and production of Canadian plays, of which there was a deplorable lack.

On February 4, 1940, Coulter gave a paper entitled "So Canadians Can't Act" over CBL radio, Toronto, in answer to a statement made by Maurice Colbourne downgrading the amateur performances of the little theatres in Canada. Coulter replied that the amateurs provided a valuable service in their revolt against old, stale conventional theater; they offered innovations and experimentations which professional theater could not afford, dependent as it is on box office receipts. The great French director Michel Saint-Denis had invited Canadian amateurs to London for professional work because they seemed to have a spontaneity the professionals lacked.

In the *Canadian Review of Music and Art* for May, 1942, ap-

peared Coulter's article "Why Sabotage the Theatre?" asking why
the war effort in the arts was directed toward giving the people such
superficial theater. He pleads for a more serious drama, directed
toward enriching the spirit, and offering first class dramatic treatment of intellectually challenging themes. He asks why government
funds are not put at the disposal of theater as they are of radio and
film, and he begs the members of the Dominion Drama Festival to
unite for this purpose to lobby for funds from the government. He
suggests that the Dominion Drama Festival change from "a gay
social occasion centering on competitive direction and acting of any
stageworthy play, to a more conscious effort to develop the theatre
as a means of interpreting . . . Canadian life and character" (6).

In 1945, the same periodical carried Coulter's article "Toward a
Canadian Theatre," which followed the now famous *Artists Brief* (for
which Coulter was partly responsible) and which had been read by
him in the House of Commons in Ottawa. As a result Canada Council was formed to aid the arts in Canada. Besides this, Coulter was
pushing the idea of a national theater similar to the Abbey Theatre
in Dublin. This article is the manifesto which he wrote to support
the movement; and it shows what a province might achieve by way
of building a national theater with workshops, library, and school,
fostering as well the writing of Canadian plays. It is a practical and
well-written document engendering enthusiasm, but Coulter's
plans never materialized in the precise form in which he presented
them, that is, as a *national* theater; his agitation, however, did lead
to the founding of the Shakespearean Festival Theatre in Stratford,
Ontario, and to theaters of the kind he advocated in Ottawa and in
several provincial capitals.

Numerous other articles were written by Coulter, chiefly in the
1940s, delineating the nature of true drama and genuine dramatic
performance. Of these, his lecture at Hart House Theatre under the
auspices of the University of Toronto Drama Committee, compares
the script writer with the genuine dramatist: the first using all the
tricks of the trade to achieve a financially successful play, the second
writing out of the inspiration and illumination of life and thereby
producing a work of art. He speaks of the plot as, "the pattern of
conduct in which the characters themselves work out their own
fulfillment" (3). An address, "Canadian Theatre," was given to the
Women's Lyceum Club, April 11, 1945. Shortly after this, in 1946,
he gave the lecture "Canada" on CBC radio for BBC, Belfast. Two

other articles both appearing in the Canadian *Saturday Night*, 1947, criticize and survey the drama material selected for the Dominion Drama Festival. The titles—"Time for Dusting Off the Drama Festival" (March 22) and "A Festival Adjudicator Should Wear Two Masks" (April 26)—plead for Canadian drama. In the March 22 article he repeats the plea he had made in the New York *Theatre Arts* in 1938 when he says:

If playwrights, actors and producers north of Niagara would turn their eyes from Broadway and look around them at a place called Canada. . . . There is inviting subject matter for plays in prairie droughts and crop-failure, in mining disasters, in the poverty of slum dwellers of city streets or country shacks but accurate reporting . . . is not enough to make a play; and indeed what is dark and grievous in the actual circumstances of life has no rightful place on the stage till it is transmuted by art into . . . the tragic experience. . . . A hundred Canadian plays are waiting for Canadians who will write them. . . . (But if there were a great Canadian play, would Canadians bother to stage it. . . . Someday the Americans or English will do it and tell us not to be ashamed). . . .

Not only did John Coulter arouse Canadians to a need for Canadian plays, teach them by his own example how to write, encourage the production of Canadian plays at the Festival and at the Arts and Letters Club to which he belonged, but he was also alert for talented Canadian writers. Very early he drew attention to the lively work of the young French Canadian dramatist Gratien Gélinas, praising his creation of Fridolin. In Gélinas, he declares, Canada has at last a theater! Aware that the *Fridolinons 46* was doing for Canada something of what the Abbey Theatre did for Ireland, Coulter saw, with great perception, that this theater could not survive outside of French Canada because an outside audience would fail to understand the mentality and nuances of reference in Quebec humor. Had Coulter been listened to, *Tit-Coq* would never have had its disastrous performance on Broadway. At the same time he appreciated what Gélinas could do for French Canada. He says of him in the Canadian *Saturday Night:*

a lively little man of inviolable artistic integrity, a superb little artist . . . scrupulously faithful to his own experience . . . possessed of such antic genius that he may yet give the world another "funny little man" as universal in appeal as is Charley Chaplin. . . . Could *Fridolinons 46* be brought to

other parts of Canada? I am afraid not. Because it would lack its French
Canadian audience, and players and audience are the two poles between
which the show sparks into light. The quick, spontaneous appreciation of
every point could not be possible outside Quebec; the players would be
chilled and the show would suffer. . . . Gélinas . . . knows that a complete
reimagining of the show in terms of the very different mentality whose
natural expression is English, is essential.

Coulter was also very impressed with a Syrian-American playwright William Saroyan for whose play *My Heart's in the Highlands*
he had written the program notes. He speaks of Saroyan's comedy as
"very naïve and immensely sophisticated. . . . Naïvete aware of its
own quality and finding fun in deploying it." Coulter sees in this
play and playwright "the . . . liveliness of a poet's imagination . . . at
play . . . restoring . . . the lost art of parable."

For several months in 1948, Coulter had a radio program called
"*Speaking as a Listener*" at CBC, Toronto, devoted to criticizing
current radio programs in Canada. Among the programs he ap-
praised were radio plays by Lister Sinclair, Joseph Schull, Len
Peterson, Tyrone Guthrie, Gratien Gélinas; programs like "The
Citizens' Forum" directed to an intelligent listening audience;
"Kindergarten of the Air," classical music with commentary by
Thomas Archer; "The Readers Take Over," a discussion between
author and readers; and "These English," a program reporting
people and places in England. His criticisms of these varied types of
radio presentations reveal an astute, critical faculty well able to
comment on radio arts and to offer constructive criticism for the
improvement of Canadian broadcasts. He ignored what he called
"the Niagara of broadcasting bilge which deluges the air all day and
nearly all night,"[3] selecting instead "a few programs with civilizing
potential." Coulter was highly stimulating in these radio criticisms,
a great crusader for true values in the use of radio by writers. He
had had experience writing criticism in Belfast some twenty years
earlier for *The Ulster Review*, describing in the memoirs this review
as "An occasional publication . . . about the . . . arts in Ulster, and
. . . the need of mutual respect and understanding of each other's
loyalties and ideals by . . . North and South in Ireland." He
criticized the radio program "2BE" in Ulster, art and art shows, and
the misuse of cinema by inartistic people. His support of genuine art
was voiced again in his CBC radio "Tribute to George Bernard

Shaw" on November 3, 1950, and in his remarks made during the interview by Charles Peaker on CBC radio in 1955.

II *Short Stories*

Although Coulter's primary interest was not in the short story, his sense of theater and experience with dramatic techniques ably fitted him for the writing of short stories. During his long life, however, he has written only a few short stories. Nine of these, worthy of review, were all the product of his early life in Belfast.

Herman Voaden, Canadian playwright and Coulter's friend, said of him that he was a superb raconteur, particularly with his group of friends at the Arts and Letters Club in Toronto. There he would be the center of attention as he described vividly and with great imagination his experiences in Ireland and England. Coulter knew how to tell a story, how to economize with words, how to lead his listeners on from one vivid scene to the next, and finally to an amusing climax, immediately drawing the story to a close. In his early life in Ulster he had written and published several short stories, beautifully crafted with clear plot and excellent characterization. He had the insight to know how to achieve that single effect in his readers so necessary to the good short story. His more outstanding stories include "Boy at a Prayer Meeting," published in *The Adelphi* in 1926, and "The Catholics Walk," "The Novice," "Dinner Hour at the Mill," "Chatterbox Walks with the Poet," "Yeats in Dublin," "The Agitator," "In the Dormitory," and "Encounter"—all of which were published in *The Ulster Review* or other Irish periodicals. A. E. (George Russell) published "Chatterbox" and "The Catholics Walk" in *The Irish Statesman*, June 28, 1924. "The Novice" was printed in *The Adelphi* and drew favorable comments. It was a short story, "Boy at a Prayer Meeting," which first drew John Middleton Murry's attention to Coulter and led, as we have seen, to his collaboration with Murry in editing *The New Adelphi*.

"Boy at a Prayer Meeting" has the single theme of a boy's introduction to manhood and the single effect of sympathy for the youngster. It is told entirely from the boy's point of view—his impressions of the shabby schoolroom where the prayer meeting is held, of the people gathered there, his fears and emotions at the sight of lovely young Miss Mable who plays the harmonium, his mother's mistaken interpretation of his excitement as evangelical enlightenment from the Holy Ghost, her proud recounting of it to the minister, Miss Mable's withdrawal with him to the attic for a piece of music, his distress, her puzzled tenderness. The story is a sensitive evocation of a boy's first love with its subsequent feelings of vexation, shame, and perplexity.

The same boy, Arthur McMaster, is the central character in "The Catholics Walk." This short story evolves around the theme of a small boy's first sight of the Fenian Procession on Saint Patrick's Day, from the Protestant schoolhouse window. Coulter gives a vivid description of the parade as seen through a small boy's eyes. Later in the evening the same boy is watching from his attic window the end of the celebrations as Catholic and Protestant come to open combat in violence in the streets. Although the story is set in the Ulster of the 1890s and presents a different picture from today's struggles, the story is not dated; it is a universal picture of the senselessness that separatists evince when prejudice is strong. Young Arthur is surprised when he discovers that some of the Fenians are Protestant: "For the first time in his life he understood that there were Protestants who were Fenians; that Catholic and rebel were not two names for the one thing" (4).

"Dinner Hour at the Mill" is a vignette of hundreds of weavers and tenters who leave their loomshares and crowd into the mill dining room for lunch. The description of the mill workers, the steaming broth and stew, the quick Irish repartee between cook and diners—all is faithfully reproduced. The writer has painted a picture for the reader to behold, rather than a story with individual characters and plot. The atmosphere is clearly one with which he is familiar and he suggests it with just the right amount of subtlety so that it seeps into the reader's subconscious mind. Many of Coulter's stories are scarcely more than vignettes but are similarly artistic in their evocation of actual times, places, and events of his early life. "William Butler Yeats in Dublin" is one of these. Coulter describes his first glimpse of Yeats on a Dublin street, his clothing and style revealing him as a poet and also as a shrewd man of affairs. He then recalls an interview he had with Yeats in Yeats' home and finally reports his observation of Yeats quietly moving about during a performance of a play at the Abbey Theatre. The total effect is one of personal recognition. A three-dimensional picture has been sketched for us, and because Coulter has that rare gift of artist turned writer, he is better able to paint an unforgettable portrait.

He has done this same thing with Canadian scenes, particularly in

"Canadian Streetcar," which was published in *Saturday Night*, August 28, 1943, and in "Muskoka Respite," published February 6, 1943. In "Canadian Streetcar" he has perceptively reproduced not only the sights and atmosphere of the five o'clock rush hour but also the indefinable reserve of the Canadian spirit. He compares the typical Canadian attitude of meek acceptance of the rigours of public transportation with the good humor of New Yorkers, the sharpness of Ulstermen, the mimicry of Dubliners, the sarcasm of Londoners. Their attitudes relieve strain and tension but the placid, timid Canadian behavior provokes only more frustration. "Muskoka Respite," in striking contrast to "Canadian Streetcar," imaginatively recreates the idyllic beauty and serenity of the northern Ontario lake country. In it he quotes Yeats as having once told him that the impulse for his poem "Innisfree" came to him in the streets of Dublin. Coulter remarks in this vignette, "I too, as I have walked in the streets of Toronto . . . have seemed to hear 'lake water lapping with low sounds by the shore.' " Coulter adds: "it may mean much that in those moments I thought, not of any of the lake shores I knew and loved so long in Ulster, but of that island in Muskoka (Dahwamah) which I saw for the first time six years ago." He describes it with the imagination of the artist giving the colors of shore and trees and blue water, comparing it with Tom Thomson's paintings—a timeless work where the frustrations of "Canadian Streetcar" are quite forgotten in a changeless succession of days. After the publication of this short piece, Coulter felt that it had little value until one afternoon while begging gas for his boat from a stranger's cottage in Lake Saint Joseph he noticed "Muskoka" framed and hanging from the cottage wall.

III *Feature Programs and Sketches*

Coulter had worked on feature radio programs while in Ulster at BBC. Among these were four series: *Down Our Street*, *Ulster Sketches*, *At the Shore*, and *Tales of the Towns*. In the first two, his work was to find in the streets, and get to the microphone or into print, working people who had some unusual quality or skill. He recognized that such work had earned for him intimate contact with the people of the Belfast back streets and country towns. The series called *At the Shore* was intended to evoke the sights and sounds, the feel, of a particular seaside place and consisted of chats with fisher folk, songs, and dramatized anecdotes. *Tales of the Towns* was similar in content but concerned with inland places and the legendary past. At the center of each was a short historic play with a musical background and folk songs. These feature programs were a highlight in Coulter's radio career in Belfast, probably because they were a mixture of the elements he loved—poetry and drama as well as fictionalized short stories and vignettes. They were pioneer work in a feature program format that is still practiced and still popular in Britain and in Ireland.

In the *The Weekly Northern Whig* and *Belfast Post* for 1931, Coulter wrote weekly serial installments entitled "Ulster Sketches." These were topographical in content with some sentimental love interest grafted on to enlist a larger audience. Actually these Ulster sketches contain some of his finest descriptive passages and are only surpassed, if surpassed at all, by the beginning chapters of his memoirs. Occasionally there is some awkward, stiff phrasing, but on the whole they evoke a vivid picture of the Ulster countryside. Crossing the Irish Sea out through the Mersey bar from Liverpool to Belfast, Coulter gives a beautiful description of passing the Isle of Man, sighting across the dark tumbling water the lights on the Ulster coast, the Copelands, the Blackhead Beacon, the far-off lights of Scotland. He uses Ulster dialogue, comparing it to a Scot's accent with its harsh clipping of consonants and broadening of vowels: "Fine boat this / Extra / She shifts along bravely / Man, she does that / She'll be in on the nick all right / What's to stop her?" The holograph copies contain many deleted passages; Coulter in this early work shows himself already his own best critic. The dialogue is an indication of what is to come in the later Ulster plays, discussed above in Chapter 2.

IV Turf Smoke

In addition to the essays, short stories, vignettes, radio feature programs, and literary criticism, Coulter has published a short novel, *Turf Smoke*, and a biography of Winston Churchill. His latest manuscript, "In My Day," his memoirs, has not been published. *Turf Smoke*, a prose version of his Irish-American play "Holy Manhattan," is in fact a better contribution in literary form than the play, which tends to be oversentimentalized Irish-American nostalgia for the "auld country." It lacks the realism and authenticity of his Ulster plays and becomes instead a watered-down version of the type of Irish-American drama that became so popular in film and on stage in the early 1940s. Possibly aware of this, Coulter rewrote it as *Turf Smoke*, a fable of two countries. It is a modest attempt to convey the loneliness of the exiled Irishman for his native country, and therefore, in a sense, Coulter's own story. It does not, however, have the literary value of his memoirs "In My Day." *Turf Smoke* is a storyteller's dramatic fable, a fictitious narrative intended to convey the true feelings of the exile. The fine pencil sketches throughout the book, which serve instead of chapter divisions and which illustrate scenes of New York and Ulster, were done by A. J. Casson, a member of the Group of Seven; the sketches have made the book a collector's item. The theme of the fable centers around the middle-aged immigrant: Coulter seems to be saying that you cannot successfully emigrate once you have reached the maturity of the late twenties or early thirties. Barney Cahill has done just that and he continues to look back at Ireland throughout his life in New York. Like Oblomov, he is the superfluous man, inactive, lazy, given to daydreams. His father had been known in Clogherbann as the laziest man on God's earth and Barney, his son, had inherited this ingenious talent. Added to this were some gifts unique to Barney, a quick-witted person, a notorious schemer, and a colorful talker, a man who, Coulter says, "manages his life as an artist manages his medium." His conversation unfortunately is not full of Ulster idioms, vivid phrases, and apt figures of speech but rather imitates the pseudo Irish-American dialect. He is the central figure of this modern fable which partakes of some of the qualities of the traditional fable—a sketch of an unusual person who becomes proverbial, a theme conveying a principle of behavior through transparent analogy, an outlook that is ironical. A typical theme for the traditional fable is the folly of never being satisfied; another is that of deserting one's own nature or calling. In structure the fable is epigrammatic and frequently ends with a significant utterance by one of the characters.

Turf Smoke has all of these characteristics. Written six years before his adaptation of "Oblomov," it was Coulter's original Irish conception of the Russian proverbial figure of indolence. The story, though realistic in detail, borders on folklore. Such a man as Barney Cahill does not exist, but his Irish counterpart lives in every first-generation Irish family in North America. It would seem that no immigrant American lives on a roof pretending he is still in Ireland by tending his rabbits and chickens, his flowering shrubs, and building there, on top of a tall building, a whitewashed cabin with a green half-door. Yet Coulter from his hotel window daily watched a man doing precisely this in New York. Through this transparent figure, Coulter makes his analogy—the typical immigrant exile can never be reconciled to life in a new country. The theme is as applicable today in the conduct of the mature Vietnamese people who now insist on returning to their own country and facing the consequences, as it was to the nineteenth- and early twentieth-century Irish immigrants. It is ironical that the immigrants, having achieved the freedom and economic security they sought, are forced by their own nostalgia for home to return to possible imprisonment and penury. *Turf Smoke* ends with a significant utterance by Barney and a bit of poetry from Monk Gibbon's poem "In Exile." Barney says that "he'd done his darndest . . . to strike the 'oul root deep and true here in the new sod . . . figuring to keep the best of the old and make the most of the new."[4] Barney's home in Clogherbann, Northern Ireland, is vividly recalled in the last lines of this fable, quoting the Monk Gibbon poem, "Who would have thought a little field, / A far-off road, a far-off lane / A far-off cottage could in time / Wake far-off thoughts with so much pain, / Wake far-off thoughts so hard to stem / A man might fear to think of them?"[5]

Why did *Turf Smoke* not become the unqualified success that was the good fortune of "Oblomov?" Possibly it was the fact that this story bordered too much on realism to become a pure fable and the dialect was too conscious an effort to imitate the Irish New Yorker. Then too, the plot is slight and unconvincing, the characters over-sentimentalized and artificial. Unconsciously the reader loses the perspective of fable and compares it unfavorably with the novel of naturalism and realism. Despite all this, the whimsy of Barney Cahill, for whom an intelligent brand of laziness has become a philosophy of life, is very appealing to the reader and one which he is apt to remember with some nostalgia. *Turf Smoke* received exceptionally good reviews in Canadian newspapers and journals when it was first published in 1945. Four years later an Irish edition was published by the Talbot Press in Dublin under the title *Turf Smoke on Manhattan*.

V Churchill

In 1944 John Coulter revised his radio play "Mr. Churchill of England," which had received favorable reviews the previous year, into the short biography *Churchill*. Published first in serial form by *Maclean's* Magazine, it was then published by the Ryerson Press, Toronto, and hailed by newspaper critics in Montreal, Ottawa, and Toronto as an original treatment of a great subject, handled with rare skill, effectively and economically highlighting the most important events in Churchill's life in a panoramic pen portrait that is extremely readable. Coulter emphasizes the character and beliefs of Winston Churchill in his loyalty to democratic principles in the political life of Great Britain. He uses for this portrayal a method called "the living newspaper technique" in which a rapid sequence of events and actual cabinet dialogue combine to make this short biography a stimulating experience. He covers events from Churchill's schooldays to his installation as prime minister in 1940, interpreting his every action as logical in the light of his early training. Much of this falls naturally into scenes, since Churchill is a dramatic personality, most of whose failures were actually delayed successes. Coulter derived his material from Churchill's own books, but he cast it in dramatic light, as only a playwright could do successfully. It is, of course, a one-sided picture since Coulter's enthusiasm for Churchill at the time of this writing is unmistakable. Nevertheless, truth is never sacrificed nor Churchill's periods of unpopularity in England diminished in any attempt to gloss over the facts. Many of Churchill's inimitable phrases and witty responses have been included so expertly that the flow of the narrative is never interrupted. The lively, vigorous style adds a new perspective to the story of this familiar and beloved figure. Coulter has used to advantage not only Churchill's own words but those of his contemporaries and of the newspaper and radio critics of that era. Added to this are Coulter's own expressive words, interpretations, and reconstructions of events. Not only the famous incidents of Churchill's colorful career but also some little-known but equally significant episodes are presented.

It is difficult to categorize this short biography as it contains elements of impressionism, realism, and epic theater in its swift-moving vignettes. The Churchill who is a symbol of the courage of the British people never overshadows Churchill, the human being. In his slow, steady growth to manhood and leadership there is nothing sudden or strange, nothing meteorlike in his rise to power. His inconsistencies are shown to be mistakes in judgment requiring change, rather than unstable movements with the tide. Coulter

clearly reveals the man who would not compromise, despite his easy
ability to change political parties; the man who often sulked but
when defeated would invariably bob to the surface again with a
renewed buoyancy, and turn to some new accomplishment; the man
who was always ready in a crisis and indeed could foresee a crisis.
The arrangement of the book follows an impressionistic pattern.
There are ten chapters, each divided into several sections of only a
page or so each, reminding one of the separate descriptions accom-
panying colored slides in an audiovisual presentation. The whole
book flows freely along with easy transitions between sections. For
example, in Chapter I, section 7, Coulter describes graphically
young Winston's near drowning in Lake Lucerne. The half page
section ends with the words, "He overtook and grasped the boat and
soon was rowing himself and his nearly exhausted friend back to
safety."[6] Section 8 begins with the words, "Safety. What and where
is safety?" This is an excellent transition from one to another of the
crises in Winston's life. Thus the book continues with picture after
picture of Churchill's career gradually unfolding until the day that
he was entrusted with Britain's life as the Nazi troops marched into
Poland, Denmark, and Norway. Coulter ends the biography with
Churchill's words: "You ask what is my policy, I will say, It is to
wage war by sea, land, and air with all our might and with all the
strength that God can give us. And to wage war against a monstrous
tyranny never surpassed in the dark, lamentable catalogue of human
crime. That is our policy. Our aim . . . is one word: Victory" (132).

VI *Memoirs*

Of all Coulter's prose, none is more engaging than his memoirs,
"In My Day." Written at eighty-seven, it represents the peak and
culmination of his unique poetic-prose style. Begun in 1973 at the
behest of his literary friends in Canada and through the courtesy of a
Canada Council grant, the memoirs were intended not only as a
compendium of his life and literary achievements, but also as a
record of the history of the revival of opera in Canada and of the
quest for a national theatre, and, in particular, of the agitation which
gave Canada its greatest artistic benefactor and patron, Canada
Council. Coulter had been one of the founding fathers of Canada
Council, so to speak, in that he had urged Canadians, almost from
the moment that he had arrived in Canada in 1936, to apply for

government aid for the arts, using the example of the British Council as a model.

"In My Day" is not simply an historical manuscript, documenting the history of the arts and Canadian drama. It is rather a richly creative autobiography of one of Canada's earliest leaders in the art of playwrighting. Because it recounts the story of a typical immigrant to Canada, it has the twofold charm of nostalgia for the old world and enthusiasm for the new. Ulster is recreated in all its beauty as it was at the end of the nineteenth century. Coulter's descriptions of the rich farmlands, the hills and mountains outside of Belfast, the peaty tussocks and dense mountain mists represent some of the finest poetic-prose writing in the memoirs. His anecdotes of family life in Belfast prove his mastery of the short story. Such experiences as having a tooth pulled, or being measured for a new suit in the Belfast of the 1890s, are narrated with dry humor and understatement. Vivid recollections, as seen through the eyes of a small, sensitive lad, of Catholics and Protestants fighting like demented savages on the streets, until soldiers with fixed bayonets sent them back to the Falls or Shankill Road, give the reader an inkling of "the troubles" in Northern Ireland as early as 1892 when John Coulter was only a four-year-old.

Then there are the colorful passages of a youngster's initiation into farm life—the sight of the ducks and geese, with their heads folded back under their feathers, at the first glimmering of dawn; the bizarre, strangely disturbing sight of the stallion mounting the black mare; the cow-in-heat being driven to the enormous cumbersome bull. Coulter describes too, his reaction to the newly invented phonograph, telephone, and motorcar; his pioneering work with the power loom as he designed a decorative tapestry. The recreation of his first glimpse of some of the great writers, artists, and politicians in Ireland and England—Yeats, Oliver Gogarty, George Bernard Shaw, G. K. Chesterton, Augustus John, Sir Winston Churchill, Eamon de Valera, Edith Sitwell, Tony Guthrie, Lennox Robinson, and a host of others—adds much to this book of memoirs.

One long idyllic passage describes his marriage, with the succeeding honeymoon to upper Ontario and the island, Dahwamah. In a letter to Coulter, John Colombo, the Canadian poet, complimented him on the exquisite prose of this section. Coulter's life with the intolerable frustrations and disappointments of the artist, he tells us, was made bearable only because of the personal happiness he and his wife experienced in each other. The account of his years in Canadian theater, radio, and television, and the founding of Canada Council are all faithfully recorded. The last decade of his life, with his return temporarily to Ireland, vividly brings home to the reader the nostalgia of the immigrant-exile for his native land.

"In My Day" is a decidedly important work for many reasons, not the least being its portrait of the artist in Canada and its depiction of Canadian drama in its gradual growth to maturity in the last forty years. As a creative prose work, it can be ranked with the best in memoir writing. An engaging style, long sentences evoking warmly imaginative scenes, the professional raconteur's ability to keep his audience interested, the playwright's gift for dramatizing events— all these talents make "In My Day" a charming contribution to Canadian literature. As a prose writer, John Coulter has combined his talents for poetry, drama, imaginative description, dialogue, storytelling, and persuasiveness in rhetoric, to produce a body of prose that is significant and astute in criticism, and artistically cre- ative in scope.

CHAPTER 8

Conclusion

THE accomplishments of John Coulter both in Ireland and England where he learned his craft, and in Canada where he applied it, distinguish him as a Canadian immigrant who bequeaths to his adopted country a rich legacy. Nathan Cohen, in a radio interview[1] in 1968, spoke as follows with Coulter:

Cohen: You're writing for a stage that doesn't exist, a theatre that doesn't exist, a theatre that rejects you. The theatre has turned you down. What loyalty do you owe to a theatre which treats you so shabbily?

Coulter: My first loyalty is not to the theatre but to myself, to what I want to say.

Cohen: But you want to write about the life you know, the life you care about, that's a life that dates back, that really relates to Ireland, and that's the theatre that wants you. So why stay in Canada?

Coulter: Because I have something to say and I want to say it here. But it is a grinding and intolerable thing.

Cohen then goes on to say that he is fascinated by two things in Coulter's life: his decision to stay in Canada and his willingness to continue to work in theater despite all the obstacles and frustrations it has brought him. Cohen said that had he lived in London, Dublin, or New York, his works would have been produced. Mavor Moore said that "His basic tragedy was that of the uprooted man."[2] Coulter himself said, "I happen to be one of those writers who is obliged to write out of my own experiences and out of my own roots. Otherwise I don't have the feeling that the thing has got the sort of authenticity necessary for me."[3]

As we have seen, Coulter began his career by using Irish folk tales and legends as the basis for his short plays. He notes in his memoirs that Sean O'Casey and Brendan Behan's parents "were of the very stuff of which plays are made."[4]. He lamented the hostility to theater in his own origins with its Puritan Protestant overtones and stiffly solemn view of life, remarking: "assuredly there is little that is theatrical about the white robes of the redeemed, unless it be that terrible concept of the washing in the Blood of the Lamb."[5]. What Coulter failed to realize was that the characteristic Ulster dourness in his Belfast family made them the perfect subjects for an Ulster play. Unwittingly he has exposed this in his delightful sketches of family and home in his recent memoirs. There are several excellent plays hidden there. His sensitive ear for the Ulster speech and Ulster idiosyncrasies would add immeasurably to the success of such plays. But it is probable that even had he written them when he first came to Canada, they would, unfortunately, not have been produced, although one cannot overlook the wide acclaim given by Canadians to his *House in a Quiet Glen*.

Nevertheless, his output in Canada has been prolific. He has, first and foremost, excelled in style, anticipating new forms of drama and offering an example of perfection in writing to younger Canadian dramatists. His chief interest was not in technique, *per se*, but in ideology and subject. He had something to say and he used theater in which to say it. He fitted his subject into whatever vessel would hold it—epic theater, realism, surrealism, impressionism, theater-of-the-absurd, verse plays, living newspaper technique, folk tales, legends, fables. He did not stay with one form long; in fact, he was a dilettante of forms, trying out first one, then another. If he could not find a form for his play, he invented one. Nathan Cohen said to him: "Your Living Newspaper technique combined the theatre of fact with the mixed media methods of presentation. There you were anticipating some very recent and important developments in stagecraft and dramaturgy, generally, just as in *Riel* you anticipated the Brechtian theory or the Piscator theory of the epic theatre. Has this been part of the trouble with getting your plays produced—that you anticipate?"[6] To this Coulter replied that it was not the form that intrigued him but the fact that "It was some particular thing I wanted to say in terms of the stage and it was the most appropriate and only way in which the thing could adequately be said. It was for that reason that I adopted the form."[7]

What did Coulter want to say? If one looks closely at some of his plays, one will notice that he is advocating a kind of socialism, explicitly in *Transit Through Fire*, implicitly in *Riel* and "Oblomov." His bitter condemnation of bigotry, particularly religious sectarian bigotry—"that rock," he says, "over which the waves of reason may break forever in vain"—is portrayed in *The Drums Are Out*, "God's Ulsterman," and *Family Portrait*. His nonconformist views can be readily perceived in "While I Live" and in his portrait of that supreme example of nonconformity—*Churchill*—as well as in the early play, *House in the Quiet Glen*. His nostalgia for home is evidenced in his choice of *Deirdre* and in "Holy Manhattan." His sensitivity to emotional problems can be seen in "Sleep, My Pretty One" and "One Weekend in Spring." His interest in monomania and megalomania is powerfully expressed in his characters—Riel, Kean, Bentham, Churchill, Bigot, Oblomov, Conochar, and McNeagh from the plays: *Riel*, "This Glittering Dust," "Laugh, Yorick, Laugh," *Churchill*, "François Bigot and the Fall of Quebec," "Oblomov," *Deirdre*, and "The Red Hand of Ulster."

Coulter is a master of technique in writing. He has a clear, fluent style for narration; he is capable of creating and sustaining atmosphere; he is economical in his use of words; he tells a good story; his poetic gift lies in rhythm and the use of imagery; he captures the nuances of Ulster speech; his dialogue is straightforward; he is skillful in description; he can make a character live.

John Colombo said of him: "Coulter has the instinct for a good subject. If born here he would not have seen the dramatic possibilities for *Riel*. . . . He made a mythic character out of *Riel*. His plays need great actors."[8] Nathan Cohen pointed out that his plays "demand large stages and large productions."[9] In the same interview, Cohen said to Coulter that *Riel* is "the play in which, in my opinion as a critic, you have done your most significant work. As a result, *Riel* has become part of the Canadian conscience." Coulter answered that he felt that *Riel* represented the revolt against subjection by subject peoples and their takeover by some powerful nation such as happened in Asia, Africa, Cuba, Latin America; the suppression of the Métis has also happened, for example, to the black people in America. In Riel he sees Martin Luther King, Ché Guevera, Fidel Castro, and Stokeley Carmichael. "The business of theatre," said Coulter, "is primarily to make the life of a community live."[10] When asked what he considered the most important aspect, he replied, "when the subject has been lifted up to the level of fable as Synge raised *Playboy of the Western World*."[11] "But it is far more difficult to make the theatre a proletarian medium," said Coulter. "Bertolt Brecht in Berlin . . . thought he had the answer but it was the highbrows who supported him, not the working people. Even in Ireland where acting is as much an instinct as an art, the working people have little interest in theatre—when translated from the marked element of theatricality in the speech and behavior of their actual life to that of plays on a stage, even lively plays about themselves such as those of O'Casey; which they ignore as not for them, but for the privileged and educated."[12]

John Coulter dedicated his life to theater in Canada, constantly advocating the writing of Canadian plays by Canadians that they might see themselves on stage, their characteristics magnified, so that a cohesive nation might develop out of this national recognition of what constitutes a Canadian. Although he was given a mixed reception—some of his plays enthusiastically received and others either rejected or neglected for long periods of time—it is to his credit that he persevered, remaining in Canada and continuing to write plays even to venerable old age. Coulter, now eighty-eight, is still actively engaged as a dramatist. If he has only partially succeeded, it may be that among the number of young Canadians writing plays today, some gifted dramatists will emerge who will continue the quest for a national theater and an intrinsically Canadian drama in Canada.

Notes and References

Chapter One

1. In a letter to this writer, February 11, 1974. The letters of Coulter quoted throughout this book are addressed to me and are in my possession except where otherwise noted; none of his letters has been published. Other letters constituting the bulk of his lifetime correspondence are in the Coulter Archives, McMaster University, Hamilton, Ontario.

2. Coulter was vindicated with a major, triumphant performance at the National Arts Centre, Ottawa, January, 1975.

3. Son of the poet, Alice Meynell. Francis Meynell was a poet, well-known typographer, and founder-owner of the famed Nonesuch Press.

4. In a letter to Coulter from Antoinette and Geoffrey Sainsbury, Colchester, Essex, England, October 9, 1967.

5. Ernest Blythe, manager of the Abbey Theatre until a few years ago. An Ulsterman enamoured of the Irish renaissance, he left his Orangemen family, went south, and learned to speak Gaelic. As a member of DeValera's Irish government after 1916, and finance minister, he was responsible for giving the Abbey Theatre its first subvention (grant). Ernest Thompson was an Orangeman and owner of a tennis court in Belfast where Coulter played.

6. Herman Voaden, interview with the writer, November 27, 1973.

Chapter Two

1. John Coulter, unpublished memoirs, "In My Day," p. 74. Since the draft-script is subject to possible changes, and is not available for consultation, only major references to pages have been given.

2. John Coulter, "The Canadian Theatre and the Irish Exemplar," *Theatre Arts Monthly* 22, no. 7 (July, 1938), 503.

3. In Coulter's interview with this writer, June 5, 1975.

4. John Coulter, *The House in the Quiet Glen* (Toronto: Macmillan, 1937), p. 24. All references to this play will be from this edition.

5. John Coulter, *Pigs*, MS, pp. 10, 11. Coulter's holograph of this and all other unpublished plays cited are in the John Coulter Archives, McMaster University, Mills Memorial Library, Special Collections, Hamilton, Ontario.

6. John Coulter, *The Family Portrait* (Toronto: Macmillan, 1937), p. 24. All quotations of this play will be taken from this edition.

7. John Coulter, "While I Live," MS, Part I, p. 24.

8. John Coulter, *The Drums Are Out* (Chicago: DePaul University Press, 1971), p. 33. All quotations from this play will be taken from this edition.

9. John Coulter, "God's Ulsterman," Part I, "Dark Days of Ancient Hate," MS, p. 6.

10. John Coulter, "God's Ulsterman," Part II, "The Red Hand of Ulster," MS, p. 35.

Chapter Three

1. Louis Riel, *London Free Press*, 1869, as quoted by Christopher Young, *Ottawa Citizen*, editorial page, January 18, 1975.

2. John Coulter, program notes to CBC-TV, *Riel*, April 23, 1961.

3. Bertolt Brecht, "Anmerkungen zur Dreigroschenoper," in *Schriften zum Theater* (Berlin: Gustav Kiepenheuer), 1931, p. 35, as quoted by Martin Esslin, *Brecht The Man and His Work* (New York: Doubleday, 1971), p. 129.

4. Bertolt Brecht, "A Short Organum for the Theatre," no. 67, translated by John Willett, *Brecht on Theatre* (New York: Hill and Wang, 1964), p. 201.

5. Bertolt Brecht, "The Good Woman of Setzuan," in *Parables for the Theatre*, trans. Eric Bentley (New York: Grove Press, 1948), p. 94.

6. John Coulter, *Riel* (Hamilton: Cromlech Press, 1972), p. 111.

7. John Colombo, "The Last Words of Louis Riel," *The Marxist Quarterly* no. 15 (Autumn, 1965), pp. 48–53.

8. Nathan Cohen, *Toronto Daily Star*, March 29, 1962, p. 20.

9. John Coulter, *CBC Times*, December 6, 1968, p. 15.

10. Herbert Whittaker, *The Globe and Mail*, November 14, 1966.

11. John Coulter, MS, "In My Day," Part II, Section 1, pp. 63, 64.

12. John Coulter, MS, "A Tale of Old Quebec."

13. David Gardner, letter to John Coulter, September 10, 1971.

14. John Coulter, MS, "In My Day," Part III, p. 135.

15. John Coulter, MS, "François Bigot and the Fall of Quebec," p. 3.

16. John Coulter, MS, "The Trial of Joseph Howe."

Chapter Four

1. John Coulter, "In My Day," MS, Part II, Section 1, p. 24.

2. In an interview with this writer at Dahwamah, Muskoka, MacTier, Ontario, June 5, 1975.

3. V. S. Pritchett, *The Living Novel* (London: Chatham, 1966), p. 233.

4. Robie Macauley, "The Superfluous Man," *Partisan Review*, 19, no. 2 (March-April, 1952), 170.

5. *Loc. cit.*

6. John Coulter, "Oblomov," MS, Act I, p. 22.

7. Nathan Cohen, *The Toronto Star*, February 13, 1959.

8. John Coulter, *The Standard Magazine* (Montreal), October 23, 1948.

9. Alexander Pope, "An Essay on Man: Epistle II," lines 63–66, in *The Poems of Alexander Pope*, ed. M. Mack (New Haven: Yale University Press, 1964), Vol. III, p. 63.

10. Bertie Scott, *The Life of Acting* (London: Bertie Scott Memorial Foundation 1953), pp. 90–95. Copies may be obtained through: Campbell Allen, 188 Goldhurst Terrace, London N.W.

11. John Coulter, introduction to the radio play, "Mr. Churchill of England," CBC, Toronto, February 3, 1943, MS, p. 1.

12. John Coulter, "Drama on Churchill," *Toronto Star*, January 3, 1942.

13. John Coulter, "In My Day," MS, Part III, p. 132.

14. William Shakespeare, *Hamlet*, ed. Hardin Craig, act V, scene 1, lines 202–213, (Chicago: Scott, Foresman & Co., 1958), p. 786.

15. John Coulter, *Laugh, Yorick, Laugh*, MS, Act I, p. 4.

16. Brian Doherty as quoted by John Coulter, "In My Day," MS, Part III, p. 133. Brian Doherty is author of the Broadway play *Father Malachi's Miracle* and founder of the Shaw Festival Theatre, Niagara-on-the-Lake.

17. John Coulter, "A Capful of Pennies," MS, Act II, p. 65.

Chapter Five

1. John Coulter, "Transit Through Fire," *News And Views of Club Programmes and Activities*, Arts and Letters Club, February, 1968.

2. Interview with Herman Voaden, Toronto, February 27, 1974.

3. Interview with Robert Weaver, Toronto, February, 1974.

4. Roger Lee Jackson, *An Historical and Analytical Study of the Origin, Development and Impact of the Dramatic Programs Produced for the English Language* (Ann Arbor: University Microfilms, 1966), p. 86.

5. John Coulter, *Radio Drama Is Not Theatre* (Toronto: Macmillan, 1937), p. 9.

6. Felix Felton (Robert Forbes Felton), *The Radio Play: Its Technique and Possibilities* (London: Sylvan Press, 1949), p. 142. Also available at CBC Reference Library, Montreal.

7. Abbot and Rider, *Handbook of Broadcasting* (New York: McGraw-Hill, 1957), p. 229.

8. In an interview with Don Mowatt, Vancouver, April 5, 1974.

9. Nathan Cohen as quoted by R. L. Jackson, p. 105.

10. In an interview with Don Eccleston, Vancouver, April 3, 1974.

11. Nathan Cohen, *Toronto Star*, February 13, 1959.

12. Mavor Moore, *Toronto Globe and Mail*, February, 1959.

13. Herbert Whittaker, *The Globe and Mail*, February, 1959.

14. Herbert Whittaker, *The Globe and Mail*, November 2, 1962.

15. Nathan Cohen, *Toronto Daily Star*, March 29, 1962.

16. In an interview with John Coulter, Toronto, October 8, 1974.

17. John Ruddy, *The Telegram* (Toronto), April 24, 1961.

Chapter Six

1. In an interview with John Coulter, Toronto, October 8, 1974.

2. Ibid.

3. Christopher Wood, "A Canadian Opera," *Canadian Review of Music and Art*, April, 1942, p. 7.

4. Augustus Bridle, "First Canadian Opera is on Air Tomorrow," *Toronto Star*, March 7, 1942.

5. Lucy Van Gogh, "New Canadian Radio Opera," *Saturday Night* March 7, 1942.

6. A. A. A., "First Masterpiece of War in Canada," *Winnipeg Free Press*, March 13, 1943.

7. "Opera by Willan-Coulter Given Review Rehearsal," *Toronto Star*, March 4, 1942.

8. John Coulter, *Transit Through Fire* (Toronto: Macmillan, 1942), Scene IV.

9. In an interview with John Coulter, Dahwamah, Ontario, June 3, 1975.

10. Healey Willan, interview, CBC radio, "Metronome," September 24, 1966.

11. Herbert Whittaker, "Libretto Swamped by Willan Score," *Globe and Mail*, September 26, 1966.

12. Lorne Betts, *Hamilton Spectator*, April 3, 1965.

13. John Coulter, "Words for Music," *Opera Canada* 6, no. 3 (September, 1965).

14. John Coulter, "Words for Music," *Theatre Arts* (1946), pp. 33, 34.

15. Ibid.

16. John Coulter, *Deirdre of the Sorrows* (Toronto: Macmillan, 1944), p. 52. All quotations from this opera will be taken from this edition.

17. John Coulter, *Deirdre of the Sorrows* (Toronto: Berandol Music Ltd. 1946). Both the vocal and full conductor's score are published here.

18. William Butler Yeats, *Plays and Controversies* (London: Macmillan, 1923), p. 33.

19. T. S. Eliot, *The Sacred Wood* (New York: Barnes and Noble, 1928), p. 60.

20. Christopher Fry, "Author's Struggle," *The New York Times*, February 6, 1955, Section II, 3:1.

21. John Coulter, "In My Day," MS, Part III, p. 73.

22. Sir Laurence Olivier as quoted by John Coulter, "In My Day," MS, Part III, p. 100.

23. Murry MacDonald as quoted by John Coulter, "In My Day," MS, Part III, p. 101.

24. *Canadian Commentator* (Toronto), May, 1961.

25. "Two Coulter Plays at Once," *Toronto Daily Star*, April 18, 1961.

26. Tyrone Guthrie, in a letter to John Coulter from London, November 25, 1952.

27. Bette Davis in a letter to John Coulter, March 8, 1960.

28. John Coulter, "Apprentice's Note for Fellow Craftsmen," in *The Blossoming Thorn* (Toronto: Ryerson Press, 1946), p. 53. All quotations will be taken from this edition.

Chapter Seven

1. John Coulter, "In My Day," MS, Part II, Section 1, p. 5.

2. John Coulter, *Books and Shows*, CBC radio, First Series, No. 1, June 16, 1942.

3. John Coulter, *Speaking as a Listener*, March 12, 1948, p. 1.

4. John Coulter, *Turf Smoke* (Toronto: The Ryerson Press, 1945), p. 186.

5. Monk Gibbon, "In Exile," as quoted by John Coulter, *Turf Smoke*, p. 187.

6. John Coulter, *Churchill* (Toronto: The Ryerson Press, 1944), p. 7.

Chapter Eight

1. Nathan Cohen, radio interview with John Coulter, December 3, 1968, on CBC Radio "Tuesday Night."

2. In an interview with Mavor Moore, York University, Toronto, February 20, 1974.

3. John Coulter, radio interview with Nathan Cohen, on CBC Radio, "Tuesday Night," December 3, 1968.

4. John Coulter, "In My Day," MS, Part III, p. 130.

5. Ibid.

6. Nathan Cohen.

7. John Coulter, interview on CBC Radio "Tuesday Night," December 3, 1968.

8. In an interview with John Colombo, Toronto, February, 1974.

9. Nathan Cohen.

10. In an interview with John Coulter, Toronto, October 8, 1974.

11. Ibid.

12. John Coulter as quoted by David Cobb, *The Telegram* (Toronto), March 18, 1967, p. 17.

Selected Bibliography

PRIMARY SOURCES

The following list includes works both published and unpublished with alternate titles in parentheses. Coulter's works may be found in the Coulter Archives, Mills Memorial Library, Special Collections, McMaster University, Hamilton, Ontario. A significant number of the plays are also in the Drama Collection, Toronto Central Library, Toronto, Ontario. The abbreviation MS signifies manuscript, TS typescript (especially of radio broadcasts).

1. Plays
"A Capful of Pennies," ("This Glittering Dust"). TS, CBC radio, Toronto, 1967.
"Christmas Comes But Once a Year." MS, 1942.
"Clogherbann Fair," ("Pigs"), ("Father Brady's New Pig"). TS, CBC radio, Toronto, 1940.
"The Crime of Louis Riel." TS, CBC radio, 1968.
The Drums Are Out. Chicago: De Paul University Press, 1971, Irish Drama Series, 6.
The Family Portrait. Toronto: Macmillan, 1937. ("The Sponger"), TS, adapted by Rita Greer Allen for CBC-TV, 1956. ("Round at Bella Neills"), ("Stars in Brickfield Street"), MS, 1937.
"François Bigot and the Fall of Quebec." TS, CBC radio, Toronto, 1970.
"God's Ulsterman" in two parts: 1. "Dark Days of Ancient Hate," 2. "The Red Hand of Ulster." TS, CBC radio, Toronto, 1974.
"Grand Old Lady of Gregor Lodge," ("Green Lawns and Peacocks"), ("While I Live"). MS, 1951.
"Holy Manhattan," ("This Is My Country"). TS, CBC radio, Toronto, 1941.
The House in the Quiet Glen and *Family Portrait.* Toronto: Macmillan, 1937.
"Laugh, Yorick, Laugh." MS, 1956.
"Mr. Churchill of England." TS, CBC radio, Toronto, 1942.
"Oblomov." MS, 1946 (stage play). "Oblomov." TS, BBC radio, 1946. "Mr. Oblomov." TS, CBC-TV, 1962.

"Quebec in 1670." TS, CBS radio, New York, 1940.
Riel. Hamilton: Cromlech Press, 1972.
"Sally's Chance." TS, BBC radio, Belfast, 1925.
"Sketch for a Portrait," ("One Weekend in Spring"). MS, 1950.
"Sleep, My Pretty One." MS, 1954, revised 1975.
"Still There's Christmas." MS, 1942.
"A Tale of Old Quebec." TS, BBC radio, London, England, 1935.
"This Great Experiment." TS, CBC radio, Toronto, 1942.
"The Trial of Joseph Howe." TS, CBC radio, Toronto, 1942.
The Trial of Louis Riel. Ottawa: Oberon Press, 1968.

2. Short Stories
"The Agitator." *Ulster Review*, 1, no. 5, (October, 1924), 108, 109.
"Boy at a Prayer Meeting." *The Adelphi*, 3, no. 12, (May, 1926), pp. 808–815.
"The Catholics Walk." *Living Age*, 323, (November 22, 1924), pp. 433–435.
"Chatterbox Walks With the Poet." *Irish Statesman*, 2, no. 16, (June 28, 1924), p. 487.
"Christmas Accordion." TS, CBC radio, 1940.
"Dinner Hour at the Mill." *Adelphi*, 10, no. 6, (September, 1935), pp. 373, 374.
"Down Our Street." *Ireland's Saturday Night*, April 16, 1936.
"Encounter." *Ulster Review*, 2, no. 9, (February, 1926), pp. 365–367.
"In the Dormitory." *Ulster Review*, 2, no. 7, (December, 1925), pp. 324–326.
"The Novice." *The New Adelphi*, 2, no. 1, (September, 1928), pp. 57, 58.
"Suburban Sketches." *Ulster Review*, 2, no. 10 (March-April, 1926), pp. 386, 387.

3. Poetry, Librettos, Biography, Novel, Correspondence, Memoirs
The Blossoming Thorn. Toronto: Ryerson Press, 1946. A book of poetry.
Churchill. Toronto: Ryerson Press, 1944. A biography published first as a serial in *Macleans* 54, nos. 8–13, April 15–July 1, 1941. April 15, pp. 16, 32, 36; May 1, pp. 2, 12, 13, 37, 38, 39, 40; May 15, pp. 17, 41–46; June 1, pp. 17, 24–30; June 15, pp. 16, 17, 37, 38; July 1, pp. 17, 29, 30, 31.
"Correspondence." MS, 1925–1975. A large collection of letters received by Coulter from various theatre personalities over a period of fifty years.
Deirdre of the Sorrows. Toronto: Macmillan, 1944. second edition, *Deirdre*. Toronto: Macmillan, 1965. Libretto for an opera.
"Fellows of Infinite Jest." MS, 1958. Dramatic poem.
"In My Day." MS, 1975. Memoirs.
"Lament for Healey Willan." *Opera Canada*, 9, no. 2, (May, 1968), pp. 17, 44. An elegy.

Transit Through Fire. Toronto: Macmillan, 1942. Libretto for an opera.
Turf Smoke, Toronto: Ryerson Press, 1945. A novel.
Turf Smoke on Manhattan. (Turf Smoke). Dublin: Talbot Press, 1949.

4. Articles, Essays, Radio Programs
"All Smoke—A Book Review." *The New Adelphi*, 3, no. 4, (June-August 1930), pp. 342, 343.
"An Evening with George Bernard Shaw." *CBC Times*, 21, no. 5, (July 13–19, 1968), pp. 6, 7.
"An Ulster Sojourn." *The Weekly Northern Whig*, Belfast, October 10 to December 12, 1931. A weekly serial of sketches.
"Art Now—Book Reviews." *The Adelphi*, 8, no. 2, (May, 1934), pp. 153, 154.
"The Art of the Playwright." MS, lecture, Hart House Theatre, University of Toronto, 1938.
"At the Shore." TS, BBC radio, Belfast, 1934. Series of sketches.
"Attention to O'Casey." *The Adelphi*, 8, no. 4, (July, 1934), pp. 278, 279.
"The Bogman." *Ulster Review* (1925).
"Book Review of the Arts." *Canadian Review of Music and Art*, 5, nos. 6, 7, p. 48.
"Books and Shows." TS, CBC radio, Toronto, June 16, 1942 to March 30, 1943. A series of reviews of books, plays and art exhibits.
"Books for the Times." TS, CBC radio, Toronto, June 19–July 10, 1945. A series of critical reviews.
"Britain's Trade and Agriculture—Review." *The Adelphi*, 4, no. 4, (July, 1932), pp. 716–718.
"Canada's Fighting Forces." TS, CBC radio, Toronto, 1942.
"Canadian Drama and the Dominion Drama Festival." TS, CBC radio, Toronto, 1941.
"Canadian National Theatre and Theatre School." Manifesto, Arts and Letters Club, MS, 1945.
"Canadian Poetry." *Canadian Review of Music and Art*, 1, no. 8, (December, 1942), pp. 15–18.
"Canadian Streetcar." *Saturday Night*, 58, no. 51, (August 28, 1943), p. 25.
"The Canadian Theatre and the Irish Exemplar." *Theatre Arts Monthly*, 22, no. 7, (July, 1938), pp. 503–509.
"The Celtic Psyche." *The Adelphi*, 4, no. 1, (April, 1932), pp. 475, 476.
"The Dominion Drama Festival in Retrospect." TS, CBC radio, Toronto, 1948.
"Dominion Drama Festival Review." TS, CBC radio, Toronto, May, 1947.
"The Drama Behind Deirdre." *The Telegram*, (Toronto), September 24, 1966, p. 7.
"The Drama in Ulster." *Ulster Review*, 2, no. 8, (January, 1926), pp. 349, 350.

"Farewell to an Irish Poet—W. B. Yeats." *The Star Weekly*, (February 18, 1939), p. 7.

"Farm and Factory." *The Adelphi*, 4, no. 2, (May, 1932), pp. 507–517.

"A Festival Adjudicator Should Wear Two Masks." *Saturday Night*, 62, no. 34, (April 26, 1947), pp. 18, 19.

"Festival in Retrospect." *Saturday Night*, 63, no. 32, (March 27, 1948), pp. 25, 36.

"Foundations—Review." *The Adelphi*, 6, no. 2, (May, 1933), pp. 142–144.

"Fridolin in English." TS, CBC radio, Toronto, 1946.

"Fridolin Plans a Show With English Idiom." *Saturday Night*, 62, no. 20, (January 18, 1947), p. 3.

"Genghis Khan—Book Review." *The Adelphi*, 12, no. 3, (June, 1936), pp. 189, 190.

"George Bernard Shaw in Dublin." TS, BBC radio, London; RTE radio, Dublin, August 13, 1958.

"The Home Counties Series." TS, BBC radio, London, 1935; CBC radio, Toronto, 1942.

"Left Wings Over Europe—Book Review." *The Adelphi*, 12, no. 6, (September, 1936), p. 384.

"Leisure in the Modern World—Reviews." *The Adelphi*, 5, no. 6, (March, 1933), pp. 464–466.

"The Living History Series." TS, CBS-WABC radio, New York, 1938.

"Machines and Men—Book Review." *The Adelphi*, 2, no. 22, (October, 1935), pp. 59, 60.

"Man and the Machine." *The New Adelphi*, 2, no. 2, (December, 1928-February, 1929), pp. 155–157.

"Manifesto: The War and the Festival Theatre in Canada." MS, 1941.

"The Mill." *The New Adelphi*, 2, no. 2, (December, 1928-February, 1929), pp. 140, 141.

"Mimicry and the Cinema." *Ulster Review*, 2, no. 8, (January, 1926), p. 347.

"The Modern Drama." *Irish Times* (1922) A series of articles.

"The Moon in the Yellow River—Play Reviews." *The Adelphi*, 6, no. 3, (June, 1933), p. 228.

"The 'More Looms' Strike." *The Adelphi*, 3, no. 6, (March, 1932), pp. 400–402.

"Much Ado About Nothing." *Ulster Review*, 2, no. 7, (December, 1925), pp. 331, 332.

"Muskoka Respite." *Saturday Night*, 58, no. 22, (February 6, 1943), p. 25.

"My Heart's in the Highlands." program note to Wm. Saroyan's play, Toronto (August 6, 1942).

"The Newer Ulster Poetry." *Ulster Review* (1926).

"Note as to the Formation of a Drama League in Ulster." MA, Belfast, 1919.

"On the Art of the Playwright." *Curtain Call*, 9, (January, 1938), p. 7.

"Other Books of Note." *The New Adelphi*, 2, no. 4, (June-August 1929), p. 379.

"Out for a Million—Book Review." *The Adelphi*, 2, no. 5, (February, 1936), p. 320.

"Penguin Books." *The Adelphi*, 12, no. 1, (April, 1936), p. 64.

"A People's Theatre." *The Adelphi*, 6, no. 4, (July, 1933), pp. 292, 293.

"Plenty or Poverty." *The Adelphi*, 4, no. 3, (June, 1932), pp. 638–640.

"Portrait of a Man." *The New Adelphi*, 2, no. 2, (May, 1931), pp. 174–176.

"Portraits and Sketches." *The Adelphi*, 10, no. 2, (May, 1935), p. 126.

Radio Drama Is Not Theatre. Toronto: Macmillan, 1937.

"Revival of the Dominion Drama Festival." *Saturday Night*, 63, no. 32, (March 22, 1948).

"Sandstone and Other Poems—Review of Anne Marriott's Poetry." *Canadian Review of Music and Art*, 4, nos. 5, 6, (April, 1946), p. 36.

"A School for Playwrights." *The New Adelphi*, 2, no. 3, (March-May, 1929), pp. 283–285.

"Shakespeare and Communism." *Ulster Review*, 2, no. 8, (January, 1926), p. 350.

"Small Stage—Book Review." *The Adelphi*, 1, no. 5, (February, 1931), p. 446.

"So Canadians Can't Act." TS, CBC radio, Toronto, (February 4, 1940).

"Some Festival Visions of National Theatre," *Saturday Night*, 62, no. 37, (May 17, 1947), pp. 20, 21.

"Speaking as a Listener." TS, CBC radio, Toronto, (March 12-May 7, 1948). Series of critical reviews.

"Suburban Sketches." *Ulster Review*, 2, no. 10, (March-April, 1926), pp. 386, 387.

"Take Thirty." TS, CBC-TV interview by Adrienne Clarkson, (November 5, 1968).

"Tales of the Towns." TS, BBC NI radio, Belfast, 1935.

"Theatre and the Massey Report: More than a Pat on the Head." *Saturday Night*, 66, no. 49, (September 11, 1951), pp. 12, 28.

"This Country in the Morning." TS, radio interview on *Riel*, CBC radio, Ottawa, (January 17, 1975).

"Those Spiritual Aristocrats." *The Adelphi*, 7, no. 6, (March, 1934), pp. 451, 452.

"Three New Plays." *Ulster Review*, 2, no. 9, (February, 1926), pp. 369, 370.

"Time for Dusting Off the Drama Festival." *Saturday Night*, 62, no. 29, (March 22, 1947), p. 22.

"Today and Tomorrow in Ulster." *Ulster Review*, (1925).

"Toward a Better Ireland." *Ulster Review*, (1925).

"Toward a Canadian Theatre." *Canadian Review of Music and Art*, 4, nos. 1, 2, (August-September, 1945), pp. 17–20.

"Turner—A Speculative Portrait—Review." *The Adelphi*, 3, no. 4, (January, 1932), p. 254.

"Twelve Months of 2BE." *Ulster Review*, 2, no. 6, (November, 1925), p. 306.

"Ulster Farmhouse Where Outlaws Once Met." *Ireland's Saturday Night,*
     (June 30–July 22, 1931). Weekly series.
"Ulster Sketches." TS, BBC radio, Belfast, 1931. Also a weekly serial, *The
     Weekly Northern Whig and Belfast Post:* "A Young Visitor's
     Impressions—Beauties of the Coastline—In the Capital," October 10,
     1931; "Belfast's Welcome—Market Day—Wonders of the Linen In-
     dustry," October 17, 1931; "Dinner Hour at the Linen Mill—Antrim
     Coast Road—Hiking Adventure," October 24, 1931; "Exploring
     Cushendall and Parkmore—In a Belfast Suburb," October 31, 1931;
     "Dinner at Malone—Visit to a Belfast Welfare Club—In the Mean
     Streets," November 7, 1931; "A Quarrel—Sabbath Evening—Twilight
     in a Garden—Legendary Figures," November 14, 1931; "Millisle and
     Greyabbey—Rehearsals and a Reconciliation," November 28, 1931; "A
     Belfast Concert and Play—The Clogher Valley—Back-o-Beyond," De-
     cember 5, 1931; "Katherine's Christmas Party—At the Giant's
     Ring—Betrothed," December 12, 1931; "Donaghadee Revelry—
     Strangford Lough and County Down—Bygone Belfast," November 21,
     1931.
"While Belfast Sleeps." *The Belfast Telegraph,* September 26-October 31,
     1931. Series of articles on the public services. "Mammoth Machine of
     Gasworks," September 26, 1931; "Where Firemen Keep Vigil," Oc-
     tober 3, 1931; "Motor—Broom Brigade," October 10, 1931; "City's
     Mechanical Brain," October 17, 1931; "Night-Time in the Royal Vic-
     toria," October 24, 1931; "Round the Harbour at Night," October 31,
     1931.
"Why Sabotage the Theatre?" *Canadian Review of Music and Art,* 1, no. 4,
     (May, 1942), pp. 5, 6, 18.
"William Butler Yeats in Dublin." *Toronto Star,* (February 12, 1939).
"Words for Music." *Opera Canada,* 6, no. 3, (September, 1965), pp. 74, 75.
"Words for Music: Confessions of a Librettist." *Theatre Arts,* 31, no. 9,
     (September, 1947), pp. 32–34.

SECONDARY SOURCES

1. Reviews of Coulter's works in general
COBB, DAVID. "The Playwright Canada Forgot," *The Telegram,* Toronto,
     (March 18, 1967), p. 17. Cobb's interview with Coulter on his life and
     works recorded faithfully and with appreciation for the "Dean of Cana-
     dian playwrights."
COHEN, NATHAN. CBC radio, *Tuesday Night,* "Interview with John Coul-
     ter," (December 3, 1968), tape at CBC radio studio, Toronto. Highly
     perceptive questioning produces answers very revealing of Coul-
     ter's philosophy and works.
DEMPSEY, MARION. "Profile: John Coulter," *Performing Arts,* 8, (Spring,
     1971), pp. 20, 21. Short summary of Coulter's life and works.

"Drama Club Invites All Canadian Plays." *Toronto Star,* (May 29, 1943), p. 12. Compliments Coulter and others at Arts and Letters Club for encouraging productions of Canadian plays.

"Dublin's Toronto Playwright." *Montreal Standard,* (October 23, 1948), 4, 22. A brief look at Coulter's dramatic career inspired by the successful production of *The Drums Are Out* at the Abbey Theatre, Dublin.

FERRY, ANTONY. "John Coulter Getting Used to Neglect," *Toronto Daily Star,* (June 11, 1960), p. 27. Short summary of Coulter's career.

"Ulster Inspired Him." *Radio Times,* Belfast, (December 24, 1954), p. 23. An account of Coulter's achievements in theatre.

2. Reviews of Individual Works

The Blossoming Thorn

ADENEY, MARCUS. "The Blossoming Thorn," *Canadian Review of Music and Art,* 5, no. 6 and 7, 1947, p. 49. Notes the patient objectivity, the precision in the use of imagery and the scope of poetic forms used.

BROWN, WILLIAM. "The Blossoming Thorn," *Canadian Forum,* 27 (September, 1947), 142. Brief analysis marking the experimental and uneven quality of the poetry.

READ, STANLEY. "The Blossoming Thorn," *Canadian Poetry,* 10, no. 3, (March, 1947), 34. Short critical review noting the delicacy and skill of the Immigrant poems and elegiac lyrics in contrast to the less successful satiric verse.

A Capful of Pennies

COHEN, NATHAN. "Capful of Pennies: It's impossible to create substance in a vacuum," *Toronto Star,* (March 23, 1967), p. 41. Sharply critical of characterizations and plot progress.

FERRY, ANTONY. "John Coulter's 17 year Obsession," *Toronto Star,* (March 20, 1967), p. 19. Records Coulter's interest in the theme of megalomania as witnessed by his plays on Louis Riel and Edmund Kean.

WHITTAKER, HERBERT. "Kean, Coulter, a Cap Full of Pennies," *The Globe and Mail,* (March 18, 1967), p. 21. Description of Kean's visit to Canada in 1826. References made also to Coulter's play.

————. "Mulcahy Evokes a Fascinating Era," *The Globe and Mail,* March 23, 1967, p. 15 Compliments Coulter on creating a pastiche of golden days in the romantic period of British theater.

Churchill

BRIDLE, AUGUSTUS. "Drama on Churchill Written in Toronto," *Toronto Star,* (January 3, 1942). Compliments Coulter on his play for its exciting use of new techniques in this saga of Churchill's life.

"Churchill." *Calgary Herald,* (June 13, 1944). Review of the biography, *Churchill,* complimenting Coulter on his vigorous, freely-running style.

"Churchill." *Ottawa Evening Journal*, (May 20, 1944). Points to the very
    readable style with which Coulter highlights the character and beliefs
    of Churchill.
"Churchill." *Toronto Star*, (May 13, 1944) 18. Brief favourable review of the
    biography.
CLARKE, GEORGE HERBERT. "Churchill," *Queens Quarterly*, 51, no. 2,
    (Summer, 1944), 206. Brief analysis of Coulter's biography of Chur-
    chill, emphasizing the intensely dramatic nature of the work, its careful
    documentation and other good qualities.
ELLIOTT, JOHN K. "Dramatic Sketch of Churchill," *London Evening Free
    Press*, (June 10, 1944). Review of the book "Churchill" with highly ap-
    preciative comments on style and substance.
M. H. E. "Churchill," *Winnipeg Free Press*, (May 27, 1944). Short review
    of the biography mentioning the colorful dialogue, the dramatic
    episodes and concise narrative style.
SMITH, M. L. "Churchill," *Dalhousie Review*, 25, no. 1, (April, 1945), p.
    120. Short review pointing out the effectiveness of the dialogue, the
    stirring dramatic qualities and strong impression of Churchill this biog-
    raphy makes on the reader.

Deirdre

ACTON, CHARLES. "An Opera from Canada," *The Irish Times*, (September
    14, 1973). Commends Coulter for a straight-forward, honest, dignified
    libretto.
ARCHER, THOMAS. "Deirdre of the Sorrows," *Radio World*, Montreal, 5,
    (May 11, 1946). Gives substantial reasons for saying that *Deirdre* set a
    new standard in operatic broadcasting.
BETTS, LORNE. "Perhaps Too Much Drama and Drive" *Hamilton Spec-
    tator*, (April 3, 1965). Criticizes Coulter's libretto which was cut for the
    stage presentation.
"Deirdre," *Newsweek*, 27, (April 29, 1946), 84. Favorable review of
    Deirdre.
"Deirdre." *Opera in Canada*, 7, no. 3, (September, 1966), p. 31. Very
    appreciative review of Coulter and Willan's work.
"Deirdre of the Sorrows." *Canadian Poetry*, 8, no. 3, (March, 1945), p. 38.
    Brief review of Coulter's libretto for the opera, *Deirdre*, congratulating
    Coulter on the simple, noble prose and verse suited to radio and the
    Irish theme.
KRAGLAND, JOHN. "Deirdre is a Triumph of Creation, Recreation," *The
    Globe and Mail*, (September 26, 1966), p. 23. Favorable review.
LITTLER, WILLIAM. "Sincere, Honest, Deirdre," *Toronto Star*, (Sep-
    tember 26, 1966), p. 20. *Deirdre*, twenty years later, is old and out of
    joint with contemporary operatic writing.
MCBRIDE, KEN. "Grand Seigneur of Canadian Music," *Opera Canada*, 6,
    no. 1, (February, 1965), pp. 7, 8. Appreciative account of the opera

Deirdre emphasizing Willan's score and Coulter's close collaboration with him.

SINCLAIR, LISTER. "Deirdre of the Sorrows," *Canadian Review of Music and Art*, 3, nos. 11, 12, (December, January, 1945), p. 42. Commends Coulter for the publication of a libretto that is an excellent dramatic poem.

SMITH, CECIL. "Lucretia and Deirdre," *Theatre Arts*, 31, no. 8, (August, 1947), pp. 10–12. Review of the CBC transcription of this year-old opera, suggesting that the poetry is too obvious even though the word rhythms and vowel values are skillfully adapted to the musical setting.

THOMAS, RALPH. "Deirdre is Fine Opera," *Toronto Daily Star*, (April 3, 1965), p. 18. Commends Coulter for a poignant libretto.

WATSON, JOHN. "Deirdre is Good Radio Opera but Also Suitable for Stage," *Saturday Night*, 61, no. 35, (May 4, 1946), p. 23. As the title indicates this writer praises the work of Coulter and Willan. He particularly notes the imagery and breadth of the figures of speech—a libretto easy to assimilate.

WHITTAKER, HERBERT. "Libretto Swamped by Willan Score," *The Globe and Mail*, (September 26, 1966), p. 23. The Coulter libretto which was cut for the stage presentation of the opera, *Deirdre*, suffered in consequence.

WINTERS, KENNETH. "Deirdre: Warmth, Tact and Quality," *Telegram*, (September 26, 1966), p. 41. Unhappy about the libretto which was cut for stage presentation.

The Drums Are Out

BROWN, BILL. "Playwright John Coulter Scored a Hit When He Brought the Orange Drums to the Heart of Eire," *The Standard Magazine*, Montreal, (October 23, 1948), pp. 4, 22. Article commending Coulter's work in Irish and Canadian theatre.

"The Drums Are Out." *Irish Tatler and Sketcher*, Dublin, 57, no. 11, (August, 1948), pp. 49, 59, 61. Very favorable review complimenting Coulter for an excellent play.

SMITH, HUGH G. "Abbey Awakens," *New York Times*, (April 25, 1948), Drama Section, p. 2 X. Complimentary review.

Family Portrait

"Ulster Playwright is Canadian Star." *The Weekly Northern Whig*, Belfast, (July 22, 1948). Description of Coulter's plays revived by the Group Theatre in Belfast.

Holy Manhattan

CHARLESWORTH, HECTOR. "Holy Manhattan," *Saturday Night*, 55, no. 28, (May 11, 1940), p. 23. Review of Coulter's play at the Arts and Letters Club, noting Coulter's gift for pungent characterization, stimulating dialogue and realistic atmosphere.

"Coulter's New Play Given Try out Here." *Toronto Star*, (May 4, 1940), p. 26. "Holy Manhattan" is described as containing good dialogue, absorbing characters and effective scenes.

House in the Quiet Glen

CRAIG, THELMA. "High Level Reached With Play Program," *The Globe and Mail*, (February 27, 1937). Enthusiastic description of *House in the Quiet Glen.*

———. "Play About Ireland Best Canadian Drama at Regional Finals," *The Globe and Mail*, (March 1, 1937). Very favorable review of Coulter's prize-winning play.

Oblomov

COHEN, NATHAN. "Passing Herd, Apathetic Play," *Toronto Star*, (February 13, 1959), p. 33. A critical review of the stage play suggesting that Coulter fails to reveal Oblomov's reasons for retiring from the world nor does he give enough of the social background to see Oblomov in the context of his times.

"The Laziest Man in Fiction: A Broadcast Version of Oblomov." *The Times*, London, (September 21, 1954), p. 11. Review of the radio play noting Coulter's craftmanship in the use of suspense.

MOORE, MAVOR. "Of Oblomofites," *The Globe and Mail*, (February 13, 1959). Points out the difficulties of the stage production at the Arts and Letters Club because it demands a great actor and because the progress of the play is from comedy to romance to tragedy. Easier to perform on radio.

WALLACE, HELEN. "Everyman's Man. Oblomov, Tickling Comedy," *The London Free Press*, Ontario, (July 12, 1967). Favorable comments on the Summer Theatre stage production of "Oblomov."

WHITTAKER, HERBERT. "Frances Hyland Shines in TV Study of Inertia," *The Globe and Mail*, (November 2, 1962), p. 9. Review of the television version noting the swift moving scenes which didn't allow for the audience to digest the situation and intention.

———. "New Regions for School Plays," *The Globe and Mail*, (February, 1959), p. 10. Discusses the Collegiate Drama Festival, the new Arts Theatre, and Coulter's stage play "Oblomov." The play receives a favorable review.

Riel

ASHLEY, AUDREY M. "Canadian Muse Satisfied in Superb Riel Performance," *The Citizen*, Ottawa, (January 14, 1975), p. 22. Review of the play.

———. "Riel a Canadian Drama in Elizabethan Terms," *The Citizen*, Ottawa, (January 11, 1975), p. 75. Interview with John Coulter on the background for the writing of his play, *Riel.*

"CBC-Tuesday Night—Interview with John Coulter." *CBC Times*, 21, no. 23, (November 30-December 6, 1968), pp. 14, 15.

COHEN, NATHAN. "Just in Passing," *Toronto Star*, (March 22, 1961), p. 18. A genuine lament that Coulter has been treated so shabbily by Toronto theater circles. Only two plays staged by non-professionals. Refers to the forthcoming TV production of *Riel*.

————. "Louis Riel Just Will Not Die," *Toronto Daily Star*, (November 24, 1966), p. 40. A sharp article chiding Canadian Theatre Circles for neglecting to produce Coulter's drama *Riel*.

————. "Riel," *Toronto Star*, (March 29, 1962), p. 20. Cohen laments that *Riel* has not been given the major production it deserves.

COLOMBO, JOHN. "A Graveyard of Good Intentions," *The Stage in Canada*, (August, 1966), pp. 6–8. Laments the fact that Canadian directors are not producing good Canadian plays such as *Riel*.

DOBBS, KILDARE. "Two Canadian Plays," *Tamarack Review*, 25, (Autumn, 1962), pp. 103–105. Favorable review of *Riel* pointing out Coulter's subtle and eloquent defense of the rights of minorities.

ENDICOTT, N. J. "John Coulter's 'Riel: A Play in Two Parts'," *University of Toronto Quarterly*, 32, (July, 1963), pp. 420, 421. Review of *Riel* in which he comments on how well Coulter unified the political and personal themes, eschewing false rhetoric and false idealization of the hero, but the heart of the drama seems too commonplace.

FERRY, ANTONY. "Riel on TV Better than Nothing But Where's the Stage Production?" *Toronto Star*, (March 25, 1961), p. 28.

GALLOWAY, MYRON. "NAC's 'Riel' Production Totally Absorbs Audience," *The Montreal Star*, (January 14, 1975), D-2. Very favorable review of the performance but some reservations about the play.

HAY, ELIZABETH. "Riel," *The Empire Advance*, Manitoba, (April 5, 1950), p. 3. Favorable review of *Riel*.

HILL, KAY. "Riel," *Canadian Authors and Bookmen*, 38, no. 2. (Winter, 1962), pp. 17, 18. Critical review of the book noting its vitality but also its lack of motivation in the characters.

JAMES, GEOFFREY. "Riel Revived," *Time*, 105, no. 5, (February 3, 1975), pp. 8, 9. A perceptive critical analysis examining the strengths and weaknesses of Coulter's play, *Riel*.

MOORE, MAVOR. "Riel Saga More Then Historical Play," *The Telegram*, Toronto, (July 6, 1960), p. 21. Successful revival in Regina cries out for a Stratford production of *Riel*.

MOSDELL, D. "Riel," *Canadian Forum*, 30, (April, 1950), p. 15. Compares *Riel* unfavorably to a tapestry—a pageant. Admits vivid characterization but laments lack of dramatic organization.

NEWMAN, RICHARD. "Telescope," *London Free Press*, Ontario, (May 2, 1961), p. 35. Regrets TV production of *Riel* being cut for two presentations.

O'BROIN, PADRAIG. "Review of 'Riel: A Play in Two Parts'," *Canadian Forum*, 42, (September, 1962), pp. 137, 138. Reviews the book and concludes that on the printed page it is not quite successful because of the number of characters and scenes. Weak in development, it is yet a moving chronicle of events at an important point in history.

PARKER, GORDON. Book Review of *Riel, The Observer*, (September 1, 1962) Complimentary review.

ROBERTSON, GEORGE. "Acting Out History," *Canadian Literature*, 14, (Autumn, 1962), pp. 73–76. Emphasizes the fact that Coulter was the first to raise Riel from contradictory history to drama. He feels it works better as a play for TV than stage, because of the numerous, short scenes. It fails to clarify Riel's essential ambiguity; yet the play is a creditable and honest dramatization.

TOVELL, VINCENT. "Review: 'Riel'," *University of Toronto Quarterly*, 20, no. 3, (April, 1951), pp. 272–274. Review of the production of *Riel* by the New Play Society in Toronto. Maintains that this play is a dramatic portrait rather than pageant or historical documentary, recording rather than interpreting *Riel*. Foresees that a production on a grand scale is needed to emphasize fully its positive qualities.

TROTT, ELIZABETH HAY. "Riel," *Leader-Post*, Regina, (April 15, 1950). Favorable review of *Riel*.

WHITTAKER, HERBERT. "Credit an Irishman for Riel Industry," *The Globe and Mail*, Toronto, (January 20, 1975), p. 14. Brief summary of Coulter's literary career with emphasis on his play, *Riel*.

———. "NAC Gives Riel a Vivid Production," *The Globe and Mail*, (January 17, 1975), p. 14. Appreciative review of the triumphant revival of *Riel* at the National Arts Center.

———. "Show Business," *The Globe and Mail*, (February 20, 1950), p. 10. Favorable review of *Riel* produced by New Play Society.

Sleep, My Pretty One

JUKES, MARY. "Once Over Lightly," *The Globe and Mail*, Toronto, (April 3, 1961), p. 12. Short summary of the history of the play with some biographical material on Coulter and his family.

MACDONALD, ROSE. "Premiere for Coulter Play," *The Telegram*, Toronto, (April 15, 1961), p. 46. Sleep—characters described as "fascinating figures in a pattern. Beethoven's 'Archduke' trio dominated the writing of the play."

MICHENER, WENDY. "Two Coulter Plays at Once," *Toronto Daily Star*, (April 18, 1961), p. 19. "Riel," the TV production, and "Sleep, My Pretty One", a stage play, are being produced the same week in Toronto. This is a short review of *Sleep*.

H. W. "Haunting Play at Centre Stage," *The Globe and Mail*, Toronto, (April 15, 1961), p. 13. Short summary of the play, its strengths and weaknesses.

Transit Through Fire
A. A. A. "First Masterpiece of War in Canada," *Winnipeg Free Press*, (March 13, 1943). "Transit" is a contribution to its genre of the first importance. Poet and composer were *en rapport*.
ADASKIN, JOHN. "Canadian Music Centre Eagerly Awaits more 'native' operas," *Opera in Canada*, 3, no. 1, (February 15, 1962), pp. 11–13. Canadian opera in retrospect—past 21 years. A large portion of article quotes John Coulter's report of *Transit Through Fire*.
BRIDLE, AUGUSTUS. "First Canada Opera is on Air Tomorrow," *Toronto Star*, (March 7, 1942), p. 28. Very descriptive. Narrates entire story and whole social philosophy.
"Opera by Willan-Coulter Given Preview Rehearsal." *Toronto Star*, (March 14, 1942), p. 22. Appreciative review of the Preview performance.
VAN GOGH, LUCY. "New Canadian Radio Opera," *Saturday Night*, 57, no. 26, (March 7, 1942), p. 16. Very favorable review noting extraordinary daring, poetic imagination, vivid eloquence, strong symbolism.
WOOD, CHRISTOPHER. "A Canadian Opera 'Transit Through Fire'," *Canadian Review of Music and Art*, 1, no. 3, (April, 1942), p. 7. On the merits of an opera written specially for radio—no thin patches in the score, rich libretto, good narrative.

Turf Smoke
CLARKE, GEORGE HERBERT. "Turf Smoke," *Queens Quarterly*, 52, no. 4, (Winter, 1945–46), pp. 493, 494. Appreciative review of Coulter's novel *Turf Smoke*, describing it as full of vitality with characters drawn with skill and understanding.
DRYSDALE, LYN V. "Bogs of Ireland," *Ottawa Citizen*, (January 12, 1946). Review of *Turf Smoke* noting the musical quality of Coulter's phrasing.
F. J. "John Coulter's First Novel Gem of Poetic Expression," *Winnipeg Tribune*, (October 13, 1945). Notes the poetic quality of the prose.
McNAUGHT, ELEANOR. "Review: 'Turf Smoke'," *Canadian Forum*, 25, (January, 1946), p. 246. Favorable review of *Turf Smoke* emphasizing Coulter's gift for creating warm, living characters.
MIDDLETON, J. E. "The Stern Activity Called Work Never Troubled Barney Cahill," *Saturday Night*, 61, no. 4, (September 29, 1945), p. 25. Short complimentary review of the novel, *Turf Smoke*, pointing out its rich humor, and love of humanity.

J. O'C. "Nostalgic Bit of Erin in Manhattan," *Halifax Chronicle Herald*, (September 29, 1945). Emphasizes the quality of Celtic imagination that makes Coulter's short novel a success.

P. P. "Clogherbann in Manhattan," *The Montreal Daily Star*, (January 5, 1946). Notes the tinge of irony in this successful fable.

C. W. "Coulter's Fable of Two Countries," *Canadian Review of Music and Art*, 4, nos. 3, 4, (December, 1945) p. 37. Remarks on the skill and economy with which Coulter tells his fable.

WOOD, CHRISTOPHER. "Through a Poet's Eyes: Irish Immigrant," *Montreal Gazette*, March 3, 1946. Congratulates Coulter on producing a short stimulating novel.

Index

173